- 2

Angel
Prayers

Angel
Prayers

Communing With Angels
to Help Restore Health,
Love, Prosperity, Joy,
and Enlightenment

JOANNE BROCAS

NEW PAGE BOOKS
A division of The Career Press, Inc.
Wayne, NJ

ANGEL PRAYERS
EDITED BY LAUREN MANOY
TYPESET BY EILEEN MUNSON
Cover art by Kim Dreyer
Printed in the U.S.A.

To order this title, please call toll-free 1-800-CAREER-1 (NJ and Canada: 201-848-0310) to order using VISA or MasterCard, or for further information on books from Career Press.

The Career Press, Inc.
220 West Parkway, Unit 12
Pompton Plains, NJ 07444
www.careerpress.com
www.newpagebooks.com

Library of Congress Cataloging-in-Publication Data
Names: Brocas, Joanne, author.
Title: Angel prayers : communing with angels to help restore health, love, prosperity, joy, and enlightenment / by Joanne Brocas.
Description: Wayne : Career Press, Inc., 2016. | Includes bibliographical references and index.
Identifiers: LCCN 2016006876 (print) | LCCN 2016009298 (ebook) | ISBN
   9781632650399 (print : alk. paper) | ISBN 9781632659590 (ebook)
Subjects: LCSH: Prayers. | Angels--Miscellanea.
Classification: LCC BL560 .B65 2016 (print) | LCC BL560 (ebook) | DDC
   202/.15--dc23
LC record available at http://lccn.loc.gov/2016006876

Dedication

To my wonderful husband and earth angel, Jock Brocas

To God and His Holy Angels—May the divine light be carried within each and every prayer for the greatest good of all who use them.

࿔

Acknowledgments

I would like to express my sincere gratitude to the following people:

- ⟡ Michael Pye, for his professionalism, sincerity, and kindness.
- ⟡ Laurie Pye, for her insight, kindness, and expertise.
- ⟡ Adam Schwartz, for his assistance, knowledge, and support.
- ⟡ Jeff Piasky for the brilliant cover design, as usual.
- ⟡ The editorial staff, who are wonderful to work with.
- ⟡ And to all of the staff at New Page Books/Career Press whom I've not personally met but who play an integral role in the production, admin, and marketing of the book.

Thank you all from my heart and soul!

Contents

*I*ntroduction

"For He shall give His angels charge over thee, to keep thee in all thy ways."

Psalms 91:11 King James Version (KJV)

The powerful words of Psalm 91:11 offer us hope, faith, guidance, protection, and celestial support. God's holy angels are assigned to each of us to help keep us in all our ways. *All of our ways* covers every conceivable moral human need that may arise. This is how loved and special we are to our omnipresent Creator.

Within our universe there exists the most extraordinary divine assistance and heavenly cosmic support that is freely made available to us at all times. All you ever need to do to receive divine intervention is to acknowledge this supreme benevolent force and then ask. The astonishing power of prayer is an essential spiritual practice that you can use to directly communicate with divine intelligence to petition help. God's holy angels play an integral role within the oneness of His Almighty Divine Power *and* intimately so within your prayer life. They belong to the highest forces of divine light and were created by God to watch over the evolution of humanity and to assist in the ongoing expansion of the entire universe.

This divinely inspired prayer book offers you direct access to God's unlimited universal power through the remarkable celestial assistance of His holy angels of divine light. These significant prayers will help to activate God's direction, wisdom, healing, and blessings in your life through the divine intervention of His holy messengers.

This delightful angel prayer book holds no intention to worship the angels in replace of the Prime Creator or to act as a substitute for your unique set of religious beliefs. It is truly intended to be a wonderful enhancement of God's divine light to your personal spiritual path, which you can also suitably adjust in ways that will best serve you. All of God's holy angels work in perfect harmony with divine truth and divine love for our greatest and highest good.

They Light Up Our Lives

There are numerous times throughout our lives when we could all do with some extra helpful guidance and support, to direct and comfort us through those difficult and trying moments. Divine assistance is always on hand, and unbeknownst to many people, the angels often send them divine light and gentle encouragement to help them gain the inner strength required to move forward. The angels are always there behind the physical scenes of our life and especially during our darkest moments, when they reach out to energetically comfort, inspire, and uplift us. They surround and infuse our body and soul with divine love and healing light imbued with divine intelligence emanating from the heart and mind of God, to help us in all our ways. These glorious celestial beings truly help us to light up our lives.

Divine Light

God's spectacular divine light is the primordial ray of Creation that is entirely imbued with absolute truth and divine love, out of which further divine qualities and attributes originate, such as beauty, grace, joy, abundance, and creativity. From this miraculous primordial ray of Creation, all other creation rays, also known as divine light frequencies, emerge and are carried within the celestial light bodies of the archangels and angels. Our souls are also birthed directly from this divine light source as we all share in the universal oneness of the divine light of God.

As sparks of pure light and divine intelligence at our spiritual core, we moved through the veil of cosmic light to find ourselves on an exciting spiritual adventure within the realms of matter. Our journey through the veil brought with it a kind of spiritual amnesia for reasons of a higher purpose. Here in the world of matter we eventually begin to awaken to a greater conscious understanding of our magnificent divine heritage, which enables us to once more realign with our original creative power. As we begin to reawaken our divine light potential within the dense lower vibration of the physical realm, the temporary veil of forgetfulness and our illusionary separation to the God consciousness within us and without us completely dissolves. The high-frequency angel prayers within this book will help you to reawaken your astonishing divine light potential so you can continuously experience greater levels of creativity to assist your life in all your ways.

This A-to-Z guide of angel prayers is especially designed to help you consciously achieve a greater harmonic resonance and realignment of your own soul's light with God's omnipotent divine power as a unified source. Your willingness to work with these high vibrational prayers will enable you to greatly increase the quantity, quality, and speed of God's divine power in your consciousness and daily life. The holy angels celebrate with joyful rapture throughout the heavenly realms whenever one of us consciously reawakens to our true divine nature. Understanding that our soul origin is one of pure love and divine light is our clear path to enlightenment.

My Journey with the Angels

From a very young age I felt a wonderfully close and natural connection to the unseen realms of light without being exposed to any outside religious influence or parental influence. Somehow I kept this conscious memory of the spiritual light alive within my heart and soul, and this awareness has never left me. At one year of age I was diagnosed with the illness meningitis and was in the hospital for many weeks. Along with very good medical care, I am certain that God's holy angels helped me to recover through the deliverance of the divine healing light. I say that I am certain because I have truly experienced this same healing light surrounding me at later stages of my life during times of trauma, operations, and illness.

My divine connection with the angels deepened and became more conscious for me around the age of four when I took to heart a beautiful "angel prayer" that we all recited at the end of each school day. I began to repeat this same angel prayer once more just before I went to sleep each night, knowing and believing that

God's angels were truly watching over me and my family: "Lord, keep us safe this night, secure from all my fears, may angels guard as while we sleep till morning light appears. Amen" (John Leland). I believe that this beautiful prayer and my acceptance and faith of the divine truth within it is another reason why I continued to keep my conscious awareness of the light within my heart and soul.

This consistent use of this special prayer set in motion a spiritual awakening of my consciousness as the veil of an illusionary separation between heaven and earth (our own God consciousness) was stripped away, and my divine alignment with the holy angels was firmly established. I was soon able to clearly hear within my intuitive mind the divine guidance of my beautiful guardian angel. Ever since that time and through the willful application of study, research, qualifications, contemplation, and meditation, the holy angels have taught me celestial insights, life lessons, and healing knowledge. They have revealed powerful teachings about the glorious effects of divine prayer, some of which I have previously shared in my other best-selling book, *The Power of Angel Medicine: Energetic Exercises and Techniques to Activate Divine Healing* (Career Press/New Page Books). The power of prayer has truly been a constant and magnificent support in my life, and this is why I was divinely inspired to offer you a wide selection of angel prayers to help enlighten, guide, heal, and support you in your daily life because they genuinely work.

How to Use This Angel Prayer Book

There are multitudes of holy angels that cover a vast variety of skills, talents, interests, and specialist attributes that all align with the will of God (Truth and Love). They include exceptional healers, divine counselors, and expert teachers of every known moral subject available to us upon the earth for us to study. The amount of divine help we can have access to is truly extraordinary, especially if you have never thought to ask for any help, guidance, and divine intervention for yourself or others up until now. You can therefore use this practical and inspirational A-to-Z angel prayer book in several different ways:

For life concerns.

You can locate your specific life concern by browsing through the A-to-Z index of angel prayers to discover the exact prayers and divine assistance you require to immediately help you. Ask, believe, and receive! (Refer to simple divine instructions further along.) You can also send divine angel prayers for others, for the animal kingdom, and for our beautiful world.

For inspiration.

You will find that each angel prayer also includes an inspirational divine light message. Therefore, you can randomly flip open to any page to receive and read the divine light message for some instant inspiration. Divine light messages are intuitively inspired writings, formulated as such after two decades of direct experience in working with the celestial energies of the angels, combined with my solid experience and background in energy healing. Each divine light message encompasses a whole host of angel assistants who work under the directive guidance of the archangel in charge. This accounts for the phrase "we angels" mentioned within any divine light message.

For soul growth.

You can meditate on and contemplate any angel prayer and divine light message. You can also keep a journal of your thoughts, feelings, ideas, divine insights, and any changes in consciousness you have become self-aware of through your ongoing daily prayer work.

For information about the angels.

Throughout the book you will discover fascinating information about many wonderful archangels, your guardian angel, and other powerful divine light forces, such as the Christ Light Consciousness and the Holy Spirit. There is duplicate information concerning the bios of these divine light beings when it comes to certain prayers because specific divine light frequencies can be and are used for numerous life issues.

For healing.

Each prayer activates a divine light frequency response from the mind of God (Absolute Truth). The holy angels then carry and deliver God's divine healing light directly to your soul. The divine light is encoded with cosmic intelligence to help make specific divine corrections and upgrades in your consciousness that will enable you to realign with the divine flow and receive all of your healing needs. For physical body healing, the divine light is used to make subtle alterations in your etheric cellular body, which is the main energetic support system for your physical body. This etheric healing work will positively help to enhance your body's physiology, strengthen your immune system, and boost your vitality.

Simple Divine Instructions

There is nothing extraordinarily difficult that you need to do when you pray. The moment you ask for divine help, intervention, guidance, a blessing, or whatever your personal request may be, a higher divine power instantly receives your request and goes to work. However, there are also some significant insights into the divine art of prayer that you may find extremely invaluable to help you get the upmost out of your prayers. Use the following three easy divine instructions to help initially guide you in your daily prayer work.

- Ask
- Believe
- Receive

Ask

Asking releases your divine petition through the act of prayer. You can always talk to God and His angels in an informal, friendly, and natural manner. Asking is more powerful when you bring all of your awareness into the present moment and you are completely mindful and sincere in saying your prayers. This allows the heart and mind to be in agreement of the desired spiritual assistance required, which will add vital power to the prayer. To help you bring your awareness into the present moment you can take a few long and slow deep breaths and begin to relax your body and mind before you begin to pray.

Asking involves the active use and responsibility of your free will. If you don't ask, you often don't get. Wishful thinking is not an act of prayer. Free will expressed at its highest potential will always be in perfect harmony with the divine law of oneness and harmlessness to all. Therefore, whatever you ask for must also harmonize with divine love and be for the greatest good of the self and the whole. Many prayers go unanswered when they do not align with these important spiritual factors. This in itself when perceived differently is also an answered prayer for the greater good.

Believe

Belief activates your faith and your faith activates God's divine intervention via His holy messengers. Believe that your prayers have been divinely received and are being dealt with behind the physical scenes of your life. This act of surrender and letting go creates the energetic space in your consciousness to receive enlightenment, guidance, healing, and support. You will notice that throughout the book each angel prayer ends with the powerful words, "Thank you. Amen. It is done!" "Thank you" releases the spiritual power of gratitude. "Amen" releases the holy divine light power through the vibratory sound of Creation. And "It is done!" releases divine faith and firm belief that your prayer has already been received, acknowledged, and answered. This combination of gratitude, creative power, and faith is truly miraculous.

Receive

You will receive answers to your prayers in agreement with your soul's plan, divine timing, and through any necessary actions that you may willfully need to address on your part. Answered prayers can therefore be instantaneous, or they may take many days, weeks, months, or even years to come to fruition. It is wise to keep in patient faith while your request is being dealt with because there are often many significant factors and forces that interplay in receiving the physical manifestation of your prayers. The truth is that for some prayers to be answered, more earth time may be necessary and required for their outcome simply because other people and other elements will need to be considered and determined. A greater synchronicity of circumstances and events may need to be set up in order for you to receive your heartfelt desires. Do not concern yourself with the time limit during this stage of prayer. Let go and let God's power and His angels go to work, while taking any necessary inspired actions on your part that will help to move you closer toward the fulfilment of what your heart and soul desires.

That's it! Enjoy the following angel prayers and continue to work with your favorite ones daily. You will soon notice positive changes manifest in your health and your life. The use of angel prayers in your daily life will help to elevate your consciousness to ascend you to a new level of light and power. This newly boosted spiritual power is exactly what you need in your present moment to live your life at your greatest creative potential.

In divine love,

Joanne Brocas

Abundance Prayer with Archangel Raphael (To help you realign with unlimited divine abundance)

"Archangel Raphael, please light up my consciousness with God's emerald green divine light frequency of His perfect abundance. I allow the light to help me release all conflict and untruth in my consciousness that interferes with my perception of abundance and of my rightful divine supply. I willingly accept and trust in God's continuous divine support and gracious abundance for my life in all my ways. I now declare God's abundance in my life with ease and grace. Thank you. Amen. It is done."

Archangel Raphael (God heals)

Archangel Raphael is typically known as God's divine healing angel who delivers God's all-powerful healing light to all who call on him for spiritual assistance. Another interpretation of his name is "God has healed," which suggests that health is already a firm reality within the mind and sight of God, and we consistently maintain this reality of perfect health within our true divine origin. Archangel Raphael's powerful divine light is therefore administered to help us to realign with our already-healed and healthy divine self. His beautiful divine light frequency also embodies the celestial qualities of divine abundance and spiritual protection during travel. He holds the complete wisdom of divine healing science within his consciousness and is therefore able to help anyone to develop and tap into their own internal divine healer, should they desire to understand the deeper truths of healing.

Divine Light Message

"The divine light of abundance is illuminating your consciousness to help you shift your inaccurate perceptions of fear, lack, and limitation back into greater harmony and flow with God's unlimited abundance. An abundance of divine light manifests upon the earth as an abundance of nature, beauty, provision, and blessings of all kinds, and is therefore not to be confused with only that of financial abundance of which most souls desire. You will soon begin to notice a greater clarity of mind as you allow celestial help to guide you in taking positive new steps in thought, faith, and action. Do not give in to the illusionary fear that life is a constant struggle as this specific physical manifestation is only a temporary blip in the grand scheme of your life. Allow us angels to enlighten your mind through the power of prayer. We will help to uplift and inspire you, and if required, to also nudge you in the direction of those who can best help you. God's light and power works through many people to bring about their deepest needs and desires. New opportunities will be presented to you that will lead you toward the abundance that is always readily available for you. You will soon be free of struggle and will overcome many energetic and material life hurdles. The quality of your consciousness is the divine key that enables you to switch on a clear channel to perceive and receive unlimited abundance in all of your ways."

Acceptance Prayer with Archangel Chamuel (To help you love, approve, and accept yourself)
"Archangel Chamuel, please light up my heart's energy center with God's rose pink divine light frequency of His perfect love. I allow the light to work deep within my heart and soul, helping me to transform my limiting thoughts and inaccurate judgments that I have carelessly formed and accepted as true about myself. I willingly choose to acknowledge that I am a perfect soul and light of God. I no longer accept the negative judgments of others about me for I know the truth of my pure divine origin. Thank you. Amen. It is done!"

Archangel Chamuel (He who sees God/He who seeks God)

Archangel Chamuel is an astonishingly radiant angel who is the beautiful embodiment of God's all-powerful divine love. His remarkable angelic service is to continuously out-ray God's divine love to all of humanity to help us overcome and rise above the illusionary fear of worldly appearances and false judgments. Divine love is at the origin of our being, and Archangel Chamuel inspires us to recognize and observe the divinity within ourselves and within all souls, and to express unconditional love for our self and others. Divine love is the most powerful cosmic force within the universe that can help to awaken us to the oneness and unity of creation, so that what we personally create is beneficial for the whole. It is the spectacular light that enables us to evolve our human souls to experience greater dimensions of light and consciousness.

Divine Light Message

"If you could spiritually observe and feel the true beauty of your own glorious soul, then you would be in perfect awe of its spectacular divine splendor. You are so much more radiant, powerful, holy, and beautiful than you could ever dream of being. The divine truth of who you are is always kept eternally blazing as a supreme light of God, shining within every cell of your spiritual anatomy from the very depths and origin of your being. You are divine in nature and your real nature is one of pure love, nothing more, nothing less. Your divine light is often temporarily dimmed and overshadowed by the ego's judgments and false illusions that you have come to hold and accept in your consciousness as true about yourself and others. It is time for you to let your light shine without further restriction and to allow divine love to resurface from the depths of your soul. Begin to love and accept yourself in accordance with divine truth, and you will soon perceive yourself and all others as beautiful divine sparks of God."

Addiction Healing Prayer with Archangel Michael
(To help spiritually support you in overcoming addiction)

"Archangel Michael, please light up my consciousness with God's royal blue divine light frequency of His perfect truth, courage, and strength of will. I am struggling with an addiction to (state addiction) and need divine help to overcome my unbalanced desires. I now willingly release my struggle, desire, and addiction over to God. I allow the divine light of truth to completely transform me, and the divine power of courage and strength to steady my will. I am ready to be fully present in my life without fear. I am ready to express the greatness of my soul without suppression. Thank you. Amen. It is done!"

Archangel Michael (He who is like God)

Archangel Michael is probably the most famous and universally known archangel of them all. His magnificent celestial body is the divine expression of God's power, absolute truth, and protection. He is depicted in great works of art as a mighty angelic being who carries a protective shield and powerful sword of light, often referred to as the "sword of truth." Some have called him a warrior angel because of the biblical reference to his casting down the fallen angel, Lucifer. Archangel Michael can help us to slay the fears of our shadow nature, to break through our illusionary limitations with the power of God's truth, and to overcome our weaknesses with divine courage and fortitude. The divine light power bestowed on this astonishing archangel by God is truly remarkable. When we reach out to him for help, he will instantly intervene and guide us through our most ardent struggles, and will divinely protect us in all our ways.

Divine Light Message

"God's almighty power is with you the moment you sincerely request divine assistance. Divine intelligence will immediately go to work in your consciousness in accordance with your heart's true desire as you have free will that we angels must honor. It is therefore important to truly desire to overcome your addiction and to keep your focus firmly on the outcome of your success, instead of upon the struggle and imbalanced desire within. The divine light will bless your soul with so much radiance and truth that you will become empowered to take positive new action. The use of daily prayer will enable you to move ever closer in overcoming your addiction(s). It is time for you to be more present and clear in your life. Nothing (no thing) has any power or control over you, for you are an exquisite courageous divine light of God. You no longer need to be controlled by fear or to suppress the glory of your soul's radiant expression within the world. When you willfully enable the reality of God's divine truth to flow though you, then the all-powerful divine light will initiate corrections in consciousness to set you free."

Alternative Therapy Prayer with Archangel Raphael
(To be divinely guided to the best/correct treatment)

"Archangel Raphael, please light my way for me to discover the best/correct alternative therapy treatment for me at this time. I am ready to receive expert guidance to help me overcome, repair, resolve, and completely heal my (name condition/issue). I release this request to you for my greatest good, knowing that divine guidance and help is coming. Thank you. Amen. It is done!"

Archangel Raphael (God heals)

Archangel Raphael is typically known as God's divine healing angel who delivers God's all-powerful healing light to all who call on him for spiritual assistance. Another interpretation of his name is "God has healed," which suggests that health is already a firm reality within the mind and sight of God, and we consistently maintain this reality of perfect health within our true divine origin. Archangel Raphael's powerful divine light is therefore administered to help us to realign with our already-healed and healthy divine self. His beautiful divine light frequency also embodies the celestial qualities of divine abundance and spiritual protection during travel. He holds the complete wisdom of divine healing science within his consciousness and is therefore able to help anyone to develop and tap into their own internal divine healer, should they desire to understand the deeper truths of healing.

Divine Light Message

"You are a glorious multidimensional spiritual being of divine consciousness that has many different levels of light bodies, energetic systems, patterns, rhythms, waves, pulsations, and flows. Your dense physical body is a result of your energy bodies of light and not prior to them. It is therefore time to take care of yourself on more than one level of your being. You are being divinely guided to the right kind of healing support and knowledge to help you regain a greater level of health and vitality. You are also being nudged to investigate more about your own remarkable spiritual anatomy so that you can overcome certain health issues that persist, which are often rooted in different aspects of your consciousness. You will discover that by working multidimensionally on all levels of your being, physical, emotional, mental, and spiritual, that you will begin to naturally empower your soul's light and awaken the divine healer within you."

Note: When you discover the therapy to help you, you can also ask Archangel Raphael to light up the consciousness of the alternative therapist to help amplify their healing work with God's divine healing power.

Ancestral/Soul Timeline Healing Prayer with Archangel Zadkiel
(To help resolve ancestor and soul timeline energetic interference)

"Archangel Zadkiel, please light up my consciousness and my ancestral timeline with God's violet divine light frequency of His perfect freedom, transformation, and transmutation. I willingly choose to forgive and release all destructive unresolved soul and ancestor memories that I still carry deep within my consciousness and cells, which interfere with my health, creative freedom, and life now. I allow the violet light to transmute the origin of this interference and to resolve all ancestral and soul timeline issues in God's perfect way, bringing freedom and transformation to all concerned. Thank you. Amen. It is done!"

Archangel Zadkiel (Righteousness of God)
Archangel Zadkiel is an extraordinary celestial angel who embodies the divine light frequency of the all-powerful violet flame and is said to be one of the seven archangels of the divine light presence of God.

The divine power of God encoded within the violet flame is truly miraculous. He is known as the archangel of God's benevolence, mercy, and memory, therefore indicating his specialized ability to locate destructive cellular memories within our timelines so they can be immediately resolved and transmuted. Archangel Zadkiel's divine light emanates with the righteousness of God, helping us to correct and transform old patterns of restrictive and destructive energies whether they be rooted in our ancestral timeline, this timeline, or from our own soul's timeline. The violet light can help to resolve and release karmic ties and other negative attachments that interfere with a person's health, vitality, and spiritual well-being.

Divine Light Message

"You are an eternal divine soul that has individuated from the heart and mind of God within the oneness of creation to experience yourself as divine love wherever you may be. You are on a fantastic cosmic journey and adventure throughout time and space, currently residing within this universe ready to express and explore your glorious divine nature in physical form. You existed before this physical embodiment and you will continue to exist after. The physical body you inhabit is partially created as such through the genetic pattern that has evolved and passed on through the generations of your particular family group. You have stored ancestor memories within your cellular system and physical DNA, as well as countless soul memories within your spiritual DNA that you bring with you to this lifetime.

Your soul's consciousness is what animates the flesh-and-blood body with your spiritual DNA. This powerful prayer will enable you to receive divine light to adjust any interference from other timelines that are unresolved so that you can be free to express more of your true divine nature without restriction. All souls are interconnected through the unifying oneness, and so each soul's frequency impacts another. As you heal generational stress, so will you positively impact your future generations. This divine light message is simply to inform you just how magnificent and complex you truly are. It is time to think much bigger and more multidimensionally, rather than only thinking from a limited physical and human perspective about your health issues and life complaints."

Animal Kingdom Prayer with Archangel Ariel
(A prayer of divine intervention and blessing for all of God's creatures)

"Archangel Ariel, please bless each and every species that make up the entirety of the animal kingdom with God's benevolent light, healing power, and love. Please intervene with your divine healing force to help protect the animals from those who negligently mistreat them, and to heal and assist any sick and injured animals in God's perfect way. May the divine light of God

mercifully support all wild and domesticated animals in all their ways. Thank you. Amen. It is done!"

Archangel Ariel (Lion of God)

Archangel Ariel is the radiant angel who is associated with healing, an overseer of nature and of the animal kingdom. His celestial healing abilities align closely with the divine light frequency of Archangel Raphael, and together they assist in the curing of disease. Archangel Ariel's name translates as "Lion of God." He is intimately connected to protecting the equilibrium balance of the earth's atmospheric conditions, including the waters of the earth. This compassionate archangel is always ready to help any sick, mistreated, or injured animals, whether they be wild or domesticated. From the birds of the air to the fish in the oceans and all kinds of animal species, Archangel Ariel's divine light is a pure benevolent force for the magnificent animal kingdom.

Divine Light Message

"We angels take the spiritual light released from your heartfelt prayer for the animal kingdom, including for your beloved pets, to help magnify God's benevolent power in their world. The love that you hold for the animals is greatly acknowledged throughout the realms of light and is also graciously accepted at a unified level of consciousness by all of God's creatures great or small. Due to your sincere love and prayers for the animals, you may find that at this time you will begin to receive wonderful visits from them in numerous

ways. From little birds, dragonflies, and butter-
flies appearing in your environment to cats, dogs,
squirrels, and so on. These special visits are their
friendly way of acknowledging your divine service, kindness, and unconditional love for them
as they come close to your energy frequency to say
hello. You may have personally requested healing
help for your pet and if so, your prayer has been
received and is being dealt with in God's perfect
way. If you have lost a dear and beloved pet, then
you can be sure that they are being totally cared
for and are loved by the angels in the heavenly
realms of light until you meet again. You may also
be considering adopting an animal as a loving pet
to offer them a sanctuary, and in return they will
offer you the greatest unconditional love you have
ever known."

Anxiety Healing Prayer with Archangel Uriel
(To help you overcome anxiety with inner peace)
*"Archangel Uriel, please light up my
consciousness with God's purple, gold, and ruby
divine light frequency of His perfect peace and
knowledge. I allow the light to help me correct
and resolve my anxious thoughts, limiting
beliefs and fearful emotions that cause me to
feel out of balance, and to replace them with
divine truth and inner peace. I willingly choose
to think peaceful thoughts, and to acknowledge*

*and amplify the divine light of peace that exists
eternally within my true divine origin. Thank you.
Amen. It is done!"*

Archangel Uriel (Light of God/Fire of God)

Archangel Uriel is one of the seven archangels of
the divine light presence whose important celestial
frequency embodies God's divine peace, ministration,
and service. This extraordinary angel is personally
involved in helping each soul to align with the Christ
Light Consciousness alight within their higher-self
nature that emanates from the greater universal current. Amplifying the light of God's wisdom within each
soul is what ultimately brings the human soul inner
peace and spiritual growth through deepened cosmic consciousness. Archangel Uriel is also known as
Saint Uriel and is often depicted in art with an open
hand holding a flame, which signifies the divine light
of God. Other symbolic associations with Archangel
Uriel include him carrying a book or scroll, representing divine light knowledge.

Divine Light Message

"The anxiety you presently hold within your consciousness and nervous system is caused by
irrational fears that often seem way beyond your
control to overcome. You are divinely equipped
through your perfect divine origin to overcome
any lower nature that has an illusionary grip over
you. Anxiety stems from a build-up of fear energy
within your vibration, which automatically suppresses the inner peace and light of the soul.
When you allow irrational fear to be in control

of your thoughts and beliefs, you set up limitations that impact the clear ability to align your mind with the Christ Light Consciousness that is kept perfectly alive within your higher-self nature at all times. The spiritual power encased within this enlightening prayer will enable you to realign your mind with the Christ Light Intelligence of your higher nature, so that divine truth can override all that is false and limiting. You will soon discover a renewed feeling of inner peace begin to blossom from deep within you, as you surrender to the power of your own divine authority to have dominion over your shadow self. You will succeed in freeing the energetic stress that has initially hindered you so that your soul's creative power can fly unlimitedly high."

B

Baby Conceiving/Fertility Prayer with Archangel Gabriel
(To help resolve fear and overcome resistance in conceiving a baby)

"Archangel Gabriel, please light up my womb with God's divine creative power to help me conceive a baby in alignment with the perfect divine timing for my soul. Divine intelligence is working God's perfect order in my physical body and overriding any dysfunctions that are interfering with my natural ability to conceive a child. I willingly release all conscious and unconscious fears to God about becoming a parent. I now surrender all of my frustrations, heartache, lack of patience, and my desperation in my desire to conceive a child to the divine light of God to be healed and resolved in His perfect way. Thank you. Amen. It is done!"

Archangel Gabriel (God is my strength)

Archangel Gabriel is a remarkable messenger angel who appears in both the Old and New Testaments of the Holy Bible, although he is not directly referred to as an archangel. Known as the angel of revelation and annunciation, Archangel Gabriel can help us to achieve clarity and purity of mind by revealing divine truth and intuitive understanding within our consciousness. Universally he is recognized as a very important divine messenger of God, especially as he announces the planned births of John the Baptist and Jesus Christ. This magnificent archangel can help us to communicate the divine light expression of our soul in a harmonious and pure manner. Archangel Gabriel is intimately connected to harmonizing the divine feminine within all souls, and his divine light frequency also assists all those who desire help with conception, pregnancy, and the welfare of children.

Divine Light Message

"Your heartfelt prayer is acknowledged by the highest forces of divine light. Your consciousness is being illuminated with divine intelligence to help you achieve your heart's desire. Many energetic influences have played their part in your wait to conceive a child. Some of these influences can be eradicated immediately, such as the unconscious fears you hold on to that can sabotage your attempts. Others involve a more intricate role, such as divine timing and soul agreements. Divine timing is always in alignment with the plans that your soul has previously agreed upon for this lifetime, with other souls. It is still possible for you to alter the arrangements you have previously made to conceive a child at a certain time in your life, if all souls agree to this plan on a higher spiritual level. Therefore, a new divine timing is set and shall be so. God always holds the perfect divine design of your physical body in Divine Mind. This powerful prayer can assist you in realigning with this perfect divine blueprint so that it is clearly out pictured within your physical body to override any dysfunctions. Keep your faith and by the power of your own divine authority know that you are well equipped to create and conceive a child."

Note: Other energetic influences concerning your partner can also interfere with your ability to conceive a child. His tension, fears, and frustrations also need to be acknowledged, resolved, and released. Men often carry the unconscious fear of not being able to financially provide for a family, and this fear can be rooted deep enough in their energy systems to interfere with conception. It takes a lot of vital energy and spiritual power to create and conceive a child. Other people and situations can also drain your vital energy and unconsciously interfere with you conceiving a baby. For this, further significant prayers are also suggested to help you: the ancestral/soul timeline healing prayer, the forgiveness prayer, and the violet flame prayer. Finally, and importantly, many souls have previously agreed to be parents and guardians of an adopted child and are therefore unable to naturally conceive because of this spiritual arrangement. This in itself brings many unique lessons and rewards. Some women do become naturally pregnant after they have adopted and honored their soul's agreement. God will always bring you the love and care of children through other routes when your desire to have your own children seems totally closed to you. Special nieces and nephews can enter into your life that you share a beautiful bond with, you may be godparents to special friend's little ones, or you may have a fulfilling career in looking after children. There is always a reason, purpose, and solution to all of life's concerns.

Baby/Child Healing Prayer with Archangel Raphael
(To help send divine healing light to yours or another's baby/child)

"Archangel Raphael, please light up my baby's/ child's (or state their name) mind, body, and soul with God's emerald green divine light frequency of His perfect healing power. Let the light enter into his/her cellular system to activate his/her own divine authority and power to heal. Please empower his/her immune system to override the illness, disease, and bodily attack for his/her greatest good. Thank you. Amen. It is done!"

Archangel Raphael (God heals)

Archangel Raphael is typically known as God's divine healing angel who delivers God's all-powerful healing light to all who call on him for spiritual assistance. Another interpretation of his name is "God has healed," which suggests that health is already a firm reality within the mind and sight of God, and we consistently maintain this reality of perfect health within our true divine origin. Archangel Raphael's powerful divine light is therefore administered to help us to realign with our already-healed and healthy divine self. His beautiful divine light frequency also embodies the celestial qualities of divine abundance and spiritual protection during travel. He holds the complete wisdom of divine healing science within his consciousness and is therefore able to help anyone to develop and tap into their own internal divine healer, should they desire to understand the deeper truths of healing.

Divine Light Message

"This unconditional healing prayer will release divine healing power to infuse, surround, and support your baby/child, or another's baby/child with the all-powerful healing light of God. We healing angels are delivering the perfect combination of divine intelligence encoded in the emerald green ray to permeate every cell of the baby/child's body and to make good that which does not best serve the baby/child. Say the prayer with firm conviction, faith, and belief that healing light is sent and will assist in their recovery in God's perfect way. God does not decide to heal one baby/child over another, and this important statement reveals that there are other significant factors involved in the re-creation of health. Each time you pray you will act as an anchor of light to help assist the baby/child in their healing repair. Divine healing light will lovingly bathe the baby/child's physical body as they sleep and will begin to rectify any imbalances within the child's energetic anatomy. All is well in the sight and mind of God, and the divine blueprint for the baby's/child's perfect health is being activated now through the brilliant power of prayer."

Blessing Prayer with Archangel Sandalphon (To ask for a divine blessing and anointing for yourself or another)

"Archangel Sandalphon, please light up my life experience with God's divine anointing and blessings of his grace, favor, and abundance. I allow the light to help support my deepest dreams and creative potential for the greatest good of the whole. I willingly choose to also be a divine blessing to others whenever the opportunity arises. I now ask for a special blessing of divine love, provision, and the anointing of personal dreams for (state name) for his/her greatest good. Thank you. Amen. It is done!"

Archangel Sandalphon (co-brother with Archangel Metatron)

Archangel Sandalphon is considered to be the prophet Elijah, who transformed his soul consciousness into the elevated status of an archangel upon entering the realms of light. He is also known as the twin or co-brother of the powerful Archangel Metatron, who was originally the human soul Enoch before he too became an archangel of cosmic consciousness. This astonishing archangel is said to be extremely tall, whose height, also symbolic for consciousness, stretches from the earth to the heavenly worlds of light. Archangel Sandalphon is known for his ability to gather the prayer requests of the faithful, to bless and arrange them in the divine light of his radiant celestial frequency, and to deliver them to God so they become empowered realized blessings for those who pray. He is also known as a master of heavenly song and is therefore associated with musical tones and vibrations, assisting in the glorious song of creation.

Divine Light Message

"You always have the ability to bless your life and the life of others through the divine power of prayer. We angels want you to know that a sincere blessing given freely from the heart and soul contains the remarkable power of divinity. By praying for yourself, you will naturally invite this divine power to anoint your creative expression, to spiritually support you, and to provide you with your physical needs and heartfelt requests. When you pray a sincere blessing of light over and for another soul, you immediately help to touch that person's consciousness with divine light and pure love that flows unhindered from the Divine. This glorious light has the power to affect the physical laws and the spiritual laws in harmony with their soul's purpose. We angels are thankful for your desire to be a beautiful channel of God's light to bless others through the creative expression of prayer and through your personal intervention in their lives. Know that your own blessings are being anointed and delivered in God's perfect way."

Breakthrough Prayer with Archangel Michael (To help you break through barriers that are holding you back)

"Archangel Michael, please light up my consciousness with God's royal blue divine light frequency of His perfect strength, courage, and truth. I allow the light of truth to help me break through the barriers of any destructive patterns of thoughts, beliefs, and behaviors that are holding me back from enabling the full creative expression of my soul. I allow the light of strength and courage to help me break free of any difficult ties and situations, so that I may receive a breakthrough into the light of new positive experiences. I willingly choose to address what needs to be faced, overcome, and dealt with for my greatest good. Thank you. Amen. It is done!"

Archangel Michael (He who is like God)

Archangel Michael is probably the most famous and universally known archangel of them all. His magnificent celestial body is the divine expression of God's power, absolute truth, and protection. He is depicted in great works of art as a mighty angelic being who carries a protective shield and powerful sword of light, often referred to as the "sword of truth." Some have called him a warrior angel because of the biblical reference to his casting down the fallen angel, Lucifer.

Archangel Michael can help us to slay the fears of our shadow nature, to break through our illusionary limitations with the power of God's truth, and to overcome our weaknesses with divine courage and fortitude. The divine light power bestowed on this astonishing archangel by God is truly remarkable. When we reach out to him for help, he will instantly intervene and guide us through our most ardent struggles, and will divinely protect us in all our ways.

Divine Light Message
"Did you know that you stand on the precipice of a breakthrough and all it takes is a leap of faith and a boost of courage to smash through the limiting barriers that have long enough held you back? Those barriers are about to exist no more in your reality as your breakthrough is imminent. We angels are helping to support you in strength of mind. We do this through encouraging your intuitive nature with positive influence, through guiding supportive people into your environment, and through revealing powerful prayers and divine knowledge to you that you can immediately begin to utilize. You are far more courageous than you may currently imagine yourself to be; courage is an aspect of your divine authentic self. This prayer will enable you to ignite divine courage from deep within you to help you overcome those temporary restrictions and difficult situations that have previously held you captive. Divine intelligence is enlightening your consciousness so you may actively use the power of your free will to make positive life changes in thought,

belief, and action. Through this potent prayer, we are helping to remove all those obstacles that no longer serve you in order that you may succeed in all your worldly endeavors. Breakthroughs of heartfelt dreams, inspirational ideas, and opportunities are inevitable."

Cancer Healing Prayer for Self with Archangel Zadkiel
(To help spiritually support you in your return to vital health)

"Archangel Zadkiel, please light up my consciousness with God's all-powerful violet light frequency of His perfect mercy, freedom, and transmutation. The violet light is now correcting and transmuting all abnormal cells, is cleaning my lymphatic system and blood stream, and is transforming the exact area of my body and psyche that is in present disharmony with my perfect original divine design. Thank you. Amen. It is done!"

Cancer Healing Prayer for Others with Archangel Zadkiel
(To help spiritually support others in their return to vital health)

"Archangel Zadkiel, please light up the consciousness of (state full name) with God's all-powerful violet light frequency of His perfect mercy, freedom, and transmutation. Send the violet light into all abnormal cells, into their lymphatic system, through their blood stream, and to the exact area of their body and psyche that is in present disharmony with their perfect original divine design. I ask that this divine prayer be for their greatest and highest good in accordance with their free will. Thank you. Amen. It is done!"

Archangel Zadkiel (Righteousness of God)

Archangel Zadkiel is an extraordinary celestial angel who embodies the divine light frequency of the all-powerful violet flame and is said to be one of the seven archangels of the divine light presence of God. The divine power of God encoded within the violet flame is truly miraculous. He is known as the archangel of God's benevolence, mercy, and memory, therefore indicating his specialized ability to locate destructive cellular memories within our timelines so they can be immediately resolved and transmuted. Archangel Zadkiel's divine light emanates with the righteousness of God, helping us to correct and transform old patterns of restrictive and destructive energies whether they be rooted in our ancestral timeline, this timeline, or from our own soul's timeline. The violet light can help to resolve and release karmic ties and other negative attachments that interfere with a person's health, vitality, and spiritual well-being.

Divine Light Message

"The violet light is a powerful divine medicine in helping you to transform any kind of anomaly in the body and psyche that is out of harmony and alignment with the perfect original divine design. When a condition such as cancer drastically depletes the vital life force of the body, there are significant applications of spiritual and energetic support that you can use to help repattern and revitalize you. Repatterning is the spiritual healing work of the divine light within the etheric cellular structure and atoms of the body. Revitalizing is the unrestricted vital life force flowing freely once more around the body, which is what empowers your astonishing immune system to work optimally. The violet light is one miraculous spiritual frequency that you can freely include in your journey of healing recovery. While it is physically necessary for you to seek medical intervention and to consume a healthy and nutritious diet to help support your immune health, it is also important for you to address your spiritual and energetic anatomy through the likes of prayer and other forms of energy treatment. Your body at this time needs a nourishing combination of divine light and vital energy to support you. This important prayer will enable the violet light to over light your spiritual and energetic anatomy in harmony with divine intelligence for your greatest good."

Note: There are other important prayers that will also be beneficial for you if you are presently experiencing a cancerous condition. These are: the ancestral/soul timeline healing prayer, the divine healing prayer, and the forgiveness prayer.

Career Change Prayer with Archangel Raziel (To help uncover your soul's talents and support you in your new career)

"Archangel Raziel, please light up my soul's talents and direct me in a career change that will be in perfect harmony with my soul's plan. Reveal to me the hidden talents of my soul so that I may activate them now for greater creative fulfillment and expression of my light. I am willing to take action and make the necessary changes I need to make to have a wonderful, fulfilling, and joyful new career. Thank you. Amen. It is done!"

Archangel Raziel (Secret of God)

This marvelous archangel is the legendary subject of the Book of the Angel Raziel, which is said to contain secret knowledge. He is imbued with remarkable divine wisdom and is the keeper of knowledge, mysteries of the world, and the secrets of God. His divine light frequency embodies all seven rays of divine light combined as one extraordinary light emanation signifying the rainbow ray. The divine light intelligence of the rainbow ray can reveal to us the divine knowledge we require to help us navigate our human soul through our physical incarnation in harmony with our life's plan. Archangel Raziel can help to illuminate our spiritual journey back into the realms of light and God consciousness.

Divine Light Message

"Through the sincere request of this specific prayer the celestial power encoded within the rainbow ray of divine light will help to reawaken the hidden talents of your soul's light. You are about to enter into a period of growth, new experiences, and an expansion of light to further amplify your unique creative expression and soul power. Your desire to discover a rewarding new career will enable us angels to guide you in the direction of wonderful new opportunities. You may be required to study for these new opportunities, or to develop some skill or talent that will be of benefit to others. Your soul is passionate about learning and experiencing new beginnings, which will help to recharge your light with radiant joy. Through this prayer you will come to recognize the opportunities for change and growth that will be beneficial and fulfilling for you. We help to encourage you to strive for the greatness that is always alive within you. Changing your career can also bring you many more blessings in your life, such as meeting new friends, moving to a new area, and doing the creative work that makes your soul sing. Sometimes the thought of change can cause you temporary fear, so keep your fortitude and faith strong and we will help you to take the leap of positive change. Know that you are being divinely guided at this time and begin to recognize the gifts and abilities that you have within you that will be of service in your satisfying new career."

Chakra Balancing Meditative Prayer with Heaven's Mighty Seven Archangels (To help rebalance, align, clear, and vitalize your chakra system)

"I ask for the pure white divine light frequency of Archangel Gabriel to light up, rebalance, and vitalize my base chakra. I ask for the violet divine light frequency of Archangel Zadkiel to light up, rebalance, and vitalize my sacral plexus chakra. I ask for the purple, gold, ruby divine light frequency of Archangel Uriel to light up, rebalance, and vitalize my solar plexus chakra. I ask for the rose pink divine light frequency of Archangel Chamuel to light up, rebalance, and vitalize my heart chakra. I ask for the royal blue divine light frequency of Archangel Michael to light up, rebalance, and vitalize my throat chakra. I ask for the emerald green divine light frequency of Archangel Raphael to light up, rebalance, and vitalize my third-eye chakra. I ask for the golden yellow divine light frequency of Archangel Jophiel to light up, rebalance, and vitalize my crown chakra. Thank you. Amen. It is done!"

Heaven's Mighty Seven Archangels

Heaven's mighty seven archangels are the seven celestial angels of the divine light presence of God. Each one of the magnificent seven is placed in energetic charge of an important divine light frequency emanating from the One primordial ray of God. These seven streams of divine light all contain unique attributes of God's creative power and are therefore also known as the rays of creation. All rays and frequencies of light are imbued with all seven colors from the One primordial ray, although the dominant color of the ray is the most prominent attribute. When we actively call upon the rays of divine light, we can truly empower our mind, body, and soul with the divine attributes of God to help us in all our ways.

Divine Light Message

"This special meditative prayer can instantly help to boost your vitality and increase your energy body with divine light. Your chakras are the gateway to your soul, your spirit, and the heavens beyond. We angels notice when your chakras are misaligned, impaired, or spinning at differing vibrations due to any emotional, psychological, spiritual, and physical ailments you are experiencing. Saying this prayer for your chakras will activate our help in placing them back into natural balance. The divine light frequencies go to work carefully within your auric field and will begin to rebalance each chakra, making sure it works in harmony with your own soul light vibration and physical body. Any physical ailments that you have or any energetic anomalies within your field will most certainly come into greater harmony and alignment with your soul's vibration, and will be rectified in accordance with your life purpose and lessons. Oftentimes our divine light work within your energy field can affect an immediate healing response. Through this prayer you may also feel us working within your energy field, which can feel like loving vibrations all around you. While you say this spiritually supportive meditative prayer, also try to focus on the specific parts of the body where the chakras are located and visualize the color associated with the archangels entering into your chakras."

Note:

The base chakra is located at the base of the spine and centered in the perineum.

The sacral plexus chakra is located just below the naval.

The solar plexus chakra is located just above the naval.

The heart chakra is located center of the chest.

The throat chakra is located center of the throat.

The third-eye chakra is located center of the forehead.

The crown chakra is located at the crown of the head.

*Christ Light Consciousness Affirmation Prayer
(To help you align with your own Christ Light
Consciousness)*
*"The Christ Light Consciousness is perfectly
expressing divine intelligence in me, through me,
and around me now. Thank you, God. Amen. It is
done!"*

The Christ Light Consciousness

The Christ Light Consciousness is the pure divine light intelligence and love that God embodies for the whole of creation that illuminates and radiates throughout the entire universe. The Christ Light Consciousness is also a spectacular aspect of every human soul, no matter what stage of spiritual awakening and maturity they are in, or what religion, if any, they are personally aligned with. The divine aspect that is known as the Christ Light Consciousness is the spark of divine presence that exists within every human soul. It is impossible to be without this God consciousness because our individual souls of light are all birthed from the One primordial ray of God's Divine Light. It is the Light of Lights that weaves us all together in the oneness of Creation. We carry God's consciousness as the higher part of our soul nature to help awaken and illuminate us, to evolve our souls in harmony with divine truth and divine love.

Divine Light Message

"The Christ Light Consciousness is awakening greater levels of divine intelligence within you to help assist your soul in your life purpose and spiritual journey. It is the most powerful of divine forces and works in all elements of your life experience with pure unconditional love. This unconditional love knows no barriers and will work for the greatest good of the whole. The Christ Light Consciousness is the pure God-force energy of your soul that was given to you upon your soul's conception. Each time you pray this divine prayer, you will draw more power and light from your own Christ Self to bless your consciousness with divine understanding. As you apply this knowledge within your daily life, you will expand the wisdom of the Christ Light Consciousness within your human soul. Know that you are on a spiritual journey of ascension and soul evolution. Divine truth is awakening within you and will soon work extraordinary miracles within your life."

Compassion Prayer with Archangel Chamuel (To help ignite your true compassionate nature)

"Archangel Chamuel, please light up my heart's energy with God's rose pink divine light frequency of His perfect love and compassion. I allow the light to dissolve all energetic barriers within my heart and consciousness that keep my true compassionate nature from shining through. I willingly choose to open my heart and expand my soul's light to express unconditional love, empathy, and compassion for myself and all others. Thank you. Amen. It is done!"

Archangel Chamuel (He who sees God/He who seeks God)

Archangel Chamuel is an astonishingly radiant angel who is the beautiful embodiment of God's all-powerful divine love. His remarkable angelic service is to continuously out-ray God's divine love to all of humanity to help us overcome and rise above the illusionary fear of worldly appearances and false judgments. Divine love is at the origin of our being, and Archangel Chamuel inspires us to recognize and observe the divinity within ourselves and within all souls, and to express unconditional love for our self and others. Divine love is the most powerful cosmic force within the universe that can help to awaken us to the oneness and unity of creation, so that what we personally create is beneficial for the whole. It is the spectacular light that enables us to evolve our human souls to experience greater dimensions of light and consciousness.

Divine Light Message

"This beautiful prayer can help you to reconnect with the true compassionate nature of your soul's light so that it can shine through once more without restriction. Energetic fields of resistance often form around a person's heart energy when they have been emotionally wounded by some painful life experiences. If the human soul is unable to heal, to let go and to soften the walls of energetic resistance, then all other heart-based frequencies of light are naturally suppressed. Compassion is a natural heart-based frequency of light that is of the soul's true divine origin. We angels will help to soften your heart's energy so that compassion can be free to blossom. We want you to understand the importance of compassionate action and feeling from within. It is the light of compassion that enables you to feel unconditional love for others. Allow yourself to heal from the painful wounds of the past and to soften your heart toward others in greater need of loving service. Feel the beating heart of compassion for them just as we angels feel loving compassion for you. You are a divine being of compassion, and we unconditionally love you."

Courage Prayer with Archangel Michael
(To help you overcome fear and tap into your inner strength)

"Archangel Michael, please light up my consciousness with God's royal blue divine light frequency of His perfect courage, strength, and truth. I allow the light to help me discover and empower the courage that is deep within my soul so that I can express the truth of my being without fear. I willingly choose to follow my heart and soul's direction, and to ignore my ego's interference and that of others. Thank you. Amen. It is done!"

Archangel Michael (He who is like God)

Archangel Michael is probably the most famous and universally known archangel of them all. His magnificent celestial body is the divine expression of God's power, absolute truth, and protection. He is depicted in great works of art as a mighty angelic being who carries a protective shield and powerful sword of light, often referred to as the "sword of truth." Some have called him a warrior angel because of the biblical reference to his casting down the fallen angel, Lucifer. Archangel Michael can help us to slay the fears of our shadow nature, to break through our illusionary limitations with the power of God's truth, and to overcome our weaknesses with divine courage and fortitude. The divine light power bestowed on this astonishing archangel by God is truly remarkable. When we reach out to him for help, he will instantly intervene and guide us through our most ardent struggles, and will divinely protect us in all our ways.

Divine Light Message

"We angels want you to know that your fear is only an earthly illusion, and that fear does not have any rule over you unless you allow it to be so. The truth of your soul is that you are a brilliant, courageous, and fearless being of love and light, and this divine aspect of you already exists within your untapped consciousness. Through this prayer we will help to chase your fears away so that you can realign with the authentic courage and strength that is your true self. You are divinely protected and held safe in our love and light. Allow the natural confidence and truth of your heart and soul to shine through. In doing so, we will help you to face and release your fear so it can be transformed into positive new energy and life. We, the angels, are empowering you with divine courage at this moment in time to assist you where you most require it. We are helping to remove the energetic interference in your life that holds you back from releasing the divine courage that is yours by birthright. We spiritually take you by the hand and will lead you to make that courageous leap of faith. The journey of your life will be a joyous one filled with love, faith, and courage."

Decree Affirmation Prayer
(I AM Divine Decrees)
(To utilize the power of your divine authority)
"I AM a perfect light of God. I AM divine
intelligence. I AM divine love. I decree through
the power of my own divine authority that I have
dominion over all earthly illusions, irrational
fears, and limitations."

The Christ Light Consciousness

The Christ Light Consciousness is the pure divine light intelligence and love that God embodies for the whole of creation that illuminates and radiates throughout the entire universe. The Christ Light Consciousness is also a spectacular aspect of every human soul, no matter what stage of spiritual awakening and maturity they are in, or what religion, if any, they are personally aligned with. The divine aspect that is known as the Christ Light Consciousness is the spark of divine presence that exists within every human soul. It is impossible to be without this God consciousness because our individual souls of light are all birthed from the One primordial ray of God's Divine Light. It is the Light of Lights that weaves us all together in the oneness of Creation. We carry God's consciousness as the higher part of our soul nature to help awaken and illuminate us, to evolve our souls in harmony with divine truth and divine love.

Divine Light Message

"You are a stunning divine aspect of the creative force that permeates all of life. This dynamic force is what empowers your authentic divine authority that you as a human soul can invoke at any time through claiming it with true command and conviction. When you begin with the words "I AM," you tap into your Christ Light Consciousness that holds the unconditional divine power you require to decree that a certain thing is so. When you say this authoritative divine decree prayer, you begin to activate the divinity within you to take back your power that you have given up to false perceptions, irrational fear, and ego control. The real divine you is a perfect light of God, imbued with all of the love and divinity that is Creation."

Distance Healing Prayer with Archangel Raphael
(To help send divine healing power to another)

"Archangel Raphael, please light up the mind, body, and soul of (state full name) with God's

*emerald green divine light frequency of His
perfect healing power. Send the divine light into
his/her cellular system and nourish every organ
of his/her body with God's vital life-force. I ask
that a divine healing change to restored health
and vitality take place within them now in God's
perfect way. I release this divine healing prayer
for their greatest good in harmony with their life's
plan. Thank you. Amen. It is done!"*

Archangel Raphael (God heals)

Archangel Raphael is typically known as God's divine healing angel who delivers God's all-powerful healing light to all who call on him for spiritual assistance. Another interpretation of his name is "God has healed," which suggests that health is already a firm reality within the mind and sight of God, and we consistently maintain this reality of perfect health within our true divine origin. Archangel Raphael's powerful divine light is therefore administered to help us to realign with our already-healed and healthy divine self. His beautiful divine light frequency also embodies the celestial qualities of divine abundance and spiritual protection during travel. He holds the complete wisdom of divine healing science within his consciousness and is therefore able to help anyone to develop and tap into their own internal divine healer, should they desire to understand the deeper truths of healing.

Divine Light Message

"There is no need for you to be in the vicinity of a person who is in need of healing to affect a physical healing change. Everything in the universe, including the physical body, consists of energy, and the reality is that energy knows no bounds concerning time and space. Although this prayer is called a distance healing prayer, there really is no distance created between the divine healing power, you, and the person needing healing assistance, especially when a sincere prayer for them has been released from your heart. We healing angels thank you for your request on behalf of another, and we lovingly bless your own soul with light in our gratitude. Divine light and healing restoration is currently unfolding in this particular situation for the greatest outcome of the person, in accordance with their free will and life plan. Perfect health and vitality is the only true reality of the divine origin of the soul's spark. The divine healing light will help to empower the consciousness of the person to harmonize with the authentic pattern of their perfect original divine design."

Divine Healing Prayer with Archangel Raphael
(To help you receive divine healing power)

"Archangel Raphael, please light up my mind, body, and soul with God's emerald green divine light frequency of His perfect healing power. I allow the light to enter into my cellular system to help correct any dysfunction in my energetic

and physical anatomy for my greatest good.
Please guide my consciousness to realign with
my perfect original divine design. I Am ready to
completely heal by resolving and correcting my
energy imbalances, and I graciously accept divine
healing now in God's perfect way. Thank you.
Amen. It is done!"

Archangel Raphael (God heals)

Archangel Raphael is typically known as God's divine healing angel who delivers God's all-powerful healing light to all who call on him for spiritual assistance. Another interpretation of his name is "God has healed," which suggests that health is already a firm reality within the mind and sight of God, and we consistently maintain this reality of perfect health within our true divine origin. Archangel Raphael's powerful divine light is therefore administered to help us to realign with our already-healed and healthy divine self. His beautiful divine light frequency also embodies the celestial qualities of divine abundance and spiritual protection during travel. He holds the complete wisdom of divine healing science within his consciousness and is therefore able to help anyone to develop and tap into their own internal divine healer, should they desire to understand the deeper truths of healing.

Divine Light Message

"Disease, physical illness, and chronic pain are often the manifested outcome of energy imbalances previously created somewhere within your mind, body, and soul that has moved out of harmony with your perfect original divine design. This powerful divine healing prayer can help you to heal in numerous ways, so that you can begin to resonate once more with the perfected energy pattern that holds vital health and well-being. God's light holds the perfect pattern of your human soul in divine mind at all times, and therefore in universal truth there is nothing to heal as at the very origin of your being you are already healthy and whole. This means that by the power of your own divine authority, you are able to reclaim your health and wholeness through the correction of your energy imbalances and the realignment to your perfected consciousness. Divine truth and divine love will be the measure by which you will harmoniously realign. We healing angels are working within your soul's light to help reveal to your consciousness where you may need to pay attention to correct and resolve some misaligned thought, belief, memory, perception, emotion, habit, and action. In doing so, you will inevitably discover a greater level of vitality, health, freedom, and radiant joy. In order to heal from disease, the body, mind, and soul must come back into balance and alignment with divine energy. Keep praying the prayer of divine healing as we work to restore the reality and truth of your divine life that is never ending and always pure."

Divine Protection Prayer with Archangel Michael
(To help invoke divine protection)

"Archangel Michael, please light up my body and soul with God's royal blue divine light frequency of His perfect divine protection. I allow the light to divinely guide and protect me in all my ways. Thank you. Amen. It is done!"

Archangel Michael (He who is like God)

Archangel Michael is probably the most famous and universally known archangel of them all. His magnificent celestial body is the divine expression of God's power, absolute truth, and protection. He is depicted in great works of art as a mighty angelic being who carries a protective shield and powerful sword of light, often referred to as the "sword of truth." Some have called him a warrior angel because of the biblical reference to his casting down the fallen angel, Lucifer. Archangel Michael can help us to slay the fears of our shadow nature, to break through our illusionary limitations with the power of God's truth, and to overcome our weaknesses with divine courage and fortitude. The divine light power bestowed on this astonishing archangel by God is truly remarkable. When we reach out to him for help, he will instantly intervene and guide us through our most ardent struggles, and will divinely protect us in all our ways.

Divine Light Message

"The moment you request divine protection it is given unto you as God has given us angels charge over you to keep you in all your ways. Divine protection forms a light of God's impenetrable force around you so that only love and spiritual light may enter and influence your intuitive nature. Divine protection involves protecting you from both physical and invisible energies that are detrimental to your soul's light, life-force, and creative power. The royal blue divine light frequency can be invoked whenever you are fearful or are in perceived danger, and as a preventive measure before you conduct any form of spiritual, healing, or physical work. You can also visualize the royal blue light surrounding you as you affirm often that you are divinely protected by the light of God. Oftentimes, through your request for divine protection, you may receive intuitive guidance to take necessary actions that will lead you away from any potential threat. A good dose of common sense, the power of prayer, and positive action are the combined ingredients for success. You may sometimes feel the celestial power of us angels around you as you notice your fearful thoughts begin to dissolve. Through the gentle touch of our light, we will bring you to that place of comfort and safety."

Ego Transformation Prayer with Archangel Raziel
(To help you transform your lower-self nature)
"Archangel Raziel, please light up my lower-self
nature with God's divine light power of knowledge
and truth that leads to ego transformation and
spiritual growth. I allow the light to help reveal
to me and shift my inaccurate perceptions into
divine truth, and to awaken my consciousness
to newer levels of spiritual understanding. I
willingly choose to integrate this new knowledge
and understanding into my daily life for my
greatest good. Thank you. Amen. It is done!"

Archangel Raziel (Secret of God)

This marvelous archangel is the legendary subject of the Book of the Angel Raziel, which is said to contain secret knowledge. He is imbued with remarkable divine wisdom and is the keeper of knowledge, mysteries of the world, and the secrets of God. His divine light frequency embodies all seven rays of divine light combined as one extraordinary light emanation signifying the rainbow ray. The divine light intelligence of the rainbow ray can reveal to us the divine knowledge we require to help us navigate our human soul through our physical incarnation in harmony with our life's plan. Archangel Raziel can help to illuminate our spiritual journey back into the realms of light and God consciousness.

Divine Light Message

"The transformation of your ego is not as difficult as you may imagine it to be for you can change your egotistical perceptions at any time, which will then result in direct positive changes in your life experience. Your ego, often known as the lower self and shadow nature, is an integral aspect of your human soul that enables you to have the free-will creative expression of your consciousness within the physical realms of reality. You are able to have and perceive many different material life experiences in numerous ways when observing from the lower-self nature. These ways often result in fear, confusion, limitation, and struggle, which bring many life lessons, until you begin to use your free-will creative power to alter your perceptions and awaken into new levels of awareness and spiritual understanding. Through this divine light prayer, you will come to understand more about the ego and overcome the shadow nature with light instead of allowing the ego to have dominating control over you. You will begin to sense the beauty of the inner light of your soul, which holds the vision of divine truth, harmony, and enlightenment. Unconditionally love and accept all aspects of you without harsh judgment and you will shine light to where it is most needed to help bring your lower self into greater harmony with divine love. The ego of the human soul is a great, wise teacher if you allow yourself to be taught by it so you can light up the shadows that are revealed to your consciousness."

Emotional Healing Prayer with Archangel Uriel
(To help you rebalance your emotional health)
"Archangel Uriel, please light up my emotional self with the perfect power of God's divine peace. I allow the light to bring peace, harmony, and resolution to the root cause of my unstable emotions and unbalanced sensitivity. I willingly choose to examine my emotional health in the light of divine truth, so that my emotions do not overwhelm me, vitally drain me, and creatively block me. Thank you. Amen. It is done!"

Archangel Uriel (Light of God/Fire of God)
Archangel Uriel is one of the seven archangels of the divine light presence whose important celestial frequency embodies God's divine peace, ministration, and service. This extraordinary angel is personally involved in helping each soul to align with the Christ Light Consciousness alight within their higher-self nature that emanates from the greater universal

current. Amplifying the light of God's wisdom within each soul is what ultimately brings the human soul inner peace and spiritual growth through deepened cosmic consciousness. Archangel Uriel is also known as Saint Uriel and is often depicted in art with an open hand holding a flame, which signifies the divine light of God. Other symbolic associations with Archangel Uriel include him carrying a book or scroll, representing divine light knowledge.

Divine Light Message

"Unbalanced emotions descend from the mental disharmony of thought, belief, and perception. While it is completely necessary for you to be able to freely experience a full range of diverse emotions for the greater benefit of the human soul experience, there are times when you allow yourself to stay stuck within them much longer than is required. This powerful emotional healing prayer will help to restore inner peace to the erratic emotions that do not serve your consciousness anymore, and which unwittingly deplete your vitality. Some of these emotions are merely triggers of an original painful event that you have judged from a human soul perspective as traumatic or negative. Whilst it is true that you may have experienced the most traumatic and painful experiences in your past, the cellular memories involved in the original event can retrigger raw emotions that lead you to relive this pain over and over again, just like it is alive in the present moment. This does not serve you in any way that is truly beneficial to your human body's vital health and your soul's creative light expression. This prayer will help to soften the edge of your sensitive nature that you have possibly come to believe is an ingrained aspect of your character. Sensitivity at its highest light expression is completely neutral, and is grounded and anchored in divine truth. This will enable a soul to stay rooted in divine peace through any difficult and trying times. And not to deny their painful emotions, suppress them, or to reenact them but to acknowledge them, feel them, accept them, forgive them, heal from them, let go of them, and move on."

Enlightenment Prayer with Archangel Jophiel
(To help you realign with your higher self)

"Archangel Jophiel, please light up my consciousness with God's golden yellow divine light frequency of His perfect wisdom, illumination, and enlightenment. I allow the light to help bring more of my higher-self nature into my conscious awareness, so I can receive further illumination, spiritual wisdom, and enlightenment along my soul's path. I willingly choose to study, contemplate, and meditate upon divine truth and divine love so that I can openly express greater levels of soul creativity and light within my life experience. Thank you. Amen. It is done!"

Archangel Jophiel (Beauty of God)

Archangel Jophiel is a radiant angel of divine light who embodies God's divine wisdom. This remarkable archangel serves to bring enlightenment to humanity to help them awaken to their own higher-self nature and their direct communion with Source energy. Archangel Jophiel's name translates as "beauty of God" because he is able to bring God's thoughts, which always contains the beauty of divine truth, directly into our consciousness to help beautify our mind, body, and soul with divine intelligence. Archangel Jophiel is one of the seven archangels of the divine light presence of God. He is considered as a prince (angel chief) of the law and guardian of divine wisdom by some traditions and is said to be a companion of Archangel Metatron.

Divine Light Message

"The journey toward enlightenment is a journey that every human soul will inevitably take. Your prayers for enlightenment have been spiritually heard, and the divine light of wisdom will always lead you to evolve your soul's light into more enlightened levels of consciousness. Like the seed in the ground that is perfectly nourished by the elements of nature, it grows to become a wondrous thing of vital strength and beauty. So does the seed of enlightenment within your consciousness grow to expand the light expression within you, to reveal ever new levels of wisdom and beauty. You are required at this time to study, contemplate, and meditate more upon divine truth to greatly assist you in your spiritual growth. The divine light of wisdom flows effortlessly into your higher-self nature, which is always in perfect harmony with the Divine Universal Mind of God. Now it is time for your conscious awareness to move into greater harmony with the enlightened nature of your beautiful higher self. Divine wisdom is ready to reveal new areas of spiritual exploration in your life in alignment with your soul's plan. Your higher self is a brilliant, dazzling, enlightened aspect of your human soul that will always help to beautify and light up your life."

F

Faith Empowerment Prayer with Archangel Faith
(To help you reignite and restore your faith)

"Archangel Faith, please light up my consciousness with God's royal blue divine light frequency of His perfect faithfulness. I allow the light to help me reignite and restore faith in myself, faith in my life purpose, and faith in my unified connection with God. I willingly choose to release all interfering doubts and to stay in the positive light of hope, belief, and faith. I know deep within my heart and soul that all is well. Thank you. Amen. It is done!"

Archangel Faith (Divine Complement of Archangel Michael)

Archangel Faith is the impressive divine feminine complement of the magnificent Archangel Michael. This delightful archangel, sometimes referred to as Archeia Faith, in reference to her feminine nature, is the grand celestial embodiment of God's unwavering faithfulness. Archangel Faith also works with the royal blue divine light frequency of God's will and truth. She is significantly important in helping humanity to keep their faith in the light of God within them to overcome all physical world illusions and struggles. Archangel Faith can help us personally to release our doubts, to surrender our fears, and to ignite our hope and faith in God's divine light intelligence.

Divine Light Message

"Faith is a beautiful divine essence that is kept eternally alive within you as the spark, spirit, and light of God. In truth the essence that is faith can never be lost, only temporarily covered by earthly illusion. This divine prayer of faith will enable you to rediscover the eternal flame of faith that has never be extinguished, only dimmed. Faith is being reignited from deep within you, and soon you will swim in an ocean of certainty that all will be well in your life without any doubt. Faith is the spiritual power to believe that this is so without your lower nature needing any firm guarantees. Just one ounce of faith is enough to allow the grander light of universal faith to wonderfully amplify the results of it within your life. Divine light is breathing new life into the situation that you believe you have lost your faith in. You have never been punished by God, overlooked, or forgotten, and you are most definitely worthy enough to be blessed in all your ways. Faith in yourself, your life's path, and the universal power of God to intervene and direct you through the eternal connection you share in the Oneness of Creation will be the light that reveals the strength of spirit within with you. This faith that is yours by divine right will surely provide you with the answers you require to overcome all of material life's blocks."

Family Harmony Healing Prayer with Archangel Chamuel (To help restore family harmony)

"Archangel Chamuel, please light up the combined consciousness of my entire family group with God's rose pink divine light frequency of His perfect love. I ask that the light help us to resolve our differences for the greatest good of the whole, restoring unconditional love, peace, and harmony throughout. I willingly choose to do my part by forgiving and releasing all judgment, blame, and criticism, and shall return my thoughts and feelings back into love and harmony. Thank you. Amen. It is done!"

Archangel Chamuel (He who sees God/He who seeks God)

Archangel Chamuel is an astonishingly radiant angel who is the beautiful embodiment of God's all-powerful divine love. His remarkable angelic service is to continuously out-ray God's divine love to all of humanity to help us overcome and rise above the illusionary fear of worldly appearances and false judgments. Divine love is at the origin of our being, and

Archangel Chamuel inspires us to recognize and observe the divinity within ourselves and within all souls, and to express unconditional love for our self and others. Divine love is the most powerful cosmic force within the universe that can help to awaken us to the oneness and unity of creation, so that what we personally create is beneficial for the whole. It is the spectacular light that enables us to evolve our human souls to experience greater dimensions of light and consciousness.

Divine Light Message

"Through the power released by this important prayer request, divine love can help to restore peace and harmony within the family group so that grievances and arguments can finally be resolved and let go. When the intention of resolution is held in the heart by just one family member, then God's light has a perfect invitation to enter into the situation and work some wonder there for the greatest good of the whole. Sometimes difficult events, upset emotions, and other external influences can cause enough disharmony within a family unit to create conflict, disagreements, and animosity that carries on. This is due to the different perceptions of the conflict held within the group and the refusal to let go of the disharmony created. There is a greater force of unconditional love that binds families together that is always in existence, even when conflict seems to temporarily subdue its power. The healing power of prayer enables families to reunite with this binding, beautiful, unconditional love so that they can move through their differences and become united again as one. Divine love is a constant, whereas conflict is temporary. God's light will work within the consciousness of each family member in harmony with their free will, so that they eventually come to realize by their own free choice that love, peace, and harmony is what brings true radiant joy to the heart and soul. Whenever you pray the healing prayer of family harmony, divine light will work within everyone's spiritual field to awaken the awareness of love, compassion, and understanding. You are truly helping to bring harmony back into the family unit."

Forgiveness Prayer with Archangel Zadkiel (To help you forgive when you are having difficulty in doing so)

"Archangel Zadkiel, please light up my mind, body, and soul with God's violet divine light frequency of His perfect transmutation, transformation, and freedom. I allow the light to help activate the divine spark of forgiveness within my heart and soul for my greatest good. Send the violet light into my painful cellular memories to help me resolve and transmute them in God's perfect way. I willingly choose to forgive myself and all others who are energetically tied to my soul so I may be free to move on and regain my radiant joy. Thank you. Amen. It is done!"

Archangel Zadkiel (Righteousness of God)

Archangel Zadkiel is an extraordinary celestial angel who embodies the divine light frequency of the all-powerful violet flame and is said to be one of the seven archangels of the divine light presence of God. The divine power of God encoded within the violet flame is truly miraculous. He is known as the archangel of God's benevolence, mercy, and memory, therefore indicating his specialized ability to locate destructive cellular memories within our timelines so they can be immediately resolved and transmuted. Archangel Zadkiel's divine light emanates with the righteousness of God, helping us to correct and transform old patterns of restrictive and destructive energies whether they be rooted in our ancestral timeline, this timeline, or from our own soul's timeline. The violet light can help to resolve and release karmic ties and other negative attachments that interfere with a person's health, vitality, and spiritual well-being.

Divine Light Message

"Forgiveness is not that easy, especially if you have been traumatically wounded and are in deep emotional pain. Other times, stubborn pride and the need to be right in an argument also prevents the heart and soul from actively forgiving. The power of this forgiveness prayer will help to open your heart energy to awaken the seed of forgiveness that is always alive within you. Whether you need to forgive yourself or others, it is time for you to truly help yourself by doing so, as the effects of this gracious act will help to restore vital health and radiant joy once more. Unforgiveness suppresses the light of your spiritual power, drains your vital energy, and can even hold you back from experiencing greater levels of joy and fulfillment. By allowing the light to work within the cellular memories of your wounds, pride, blame, and guilt, you will eventually come to gain true freedom of the human soul and evolve your consciousness. Forgiveness will help you to release energetic ties that can keep you karmically bonded long after this physical life ends. By allowing yourself to forgive without conditions, you will sever these karmic ties and release all souls involved to move on and evolve their consciousness in their own time. Forgiveness is therefore an act that truly serves and blesses you, if you allow it entry. The power of the violet light, along with the Christ Light Consciousness, can help you to forgive when you are having difficulty in doing so alone. Be gentle, kind, and patient with yourself as you say the prayer often, and soon you will begin to witness the act of forgiveness has already happened."

G

Grief Healing Prayer with Archangel Raphael
(To help you move through your journey of grief)
"Archangel Raphael, please light up my heart
and soul with God's emerald green divine light
frequency of His perfect healing power. I accept
the light to help support me through my painful
loss, thoughts, and emotions. Please comfort and
restore me in God's perfect healing way. I know
that love is eternal and our souls will surely meet
again in joyful reunion within the realms of light.
Thank you. Amen. It is done!"

Archangel Raphael (God heals)

Archangel Raphael is typically known as God's divine healing angel who delivers God's all-powerful healing light to all who call on him for spiritual assistance. Another interpretation of his name is "God has healed," which suggests that health is already a firm reality within the mind and sight of God, and we consistently maintain this reality of perfect health within our true divine origin. Archangel Raphael's powerful divine light is therefore administered to help us to realign with our already-healed and healthy divine self. His beautiful divine light frequency also embodies the celestial qualities of divine abundance and spiritual protection during travel. He holds the complete wisdom of divine healing science within his consciousness and is therefore able to help anyone to develop and tap into their own internal divine healer, should they desire to understand the deeper truths of healing.

Divine Light Message

"Through this divine healing prayer you will immediately receive divine love and light to help comfort and support you in your time of need. You are being lovingly held in high vibrational energies to enable you to feel safe to release your deep inner sadness and continue your journey through grief. You may find that at this time you will receive tangible signs of us angels around you as we bring you symbolic word that your loved one is safe and sound in the glorious realms of light. A small bird, a butterfly, a special song, or a white feather are just some of these signs. We angels feel your emotional pain, and we do what we can to help ease it without interfering in your primal need to release your grief. Know that you are not alone at this difficult time, and through our influence we will also send those who can be of physical support and comfort to you. Please do talk to us about your feelings at any time as we are always ready to listen and intervene. You are deeply loved by God and a higher power, and when you cry your silent tears of sadness, we angels take your tears and turn them into sparks of light to help uplift you. We can assure you that love is eternal, and in time you will meet again with your loved one in the magnificent realms of light. We carry their love as bursts of light directly to your soul, so that you can feel the familiar energy that beautifully unites you together. Your loved one receives the kisses you send them; they hear what you tell them, and they deeply feel the love you have for them. They draw close to your consciousness and wish you to know that their heart's desire for you is to succeed and win through, to make the most out of the rest of your life so that they can celebrate your wonderful life with you. They are the feeling of warmth in your heart, the song you hear in your ear, and the gentle breeze that comes around you. You are eternally connected throughout cosmic consciousness."

*Grounding Prayer with Archangel Gabriel
(To help you ground your energies into the
present moment)*
"Archangel Gabriel, please help me to ground
my consciousness into my body and within this
present moment for my greatest good. I allow the
white light of purity and vitality to radiate through
me to help me regain balance of my energies in
my daily life. I willingly choose to be fully present
to my thoughts, feelings, and actions so that I

can take greater responsibility and become more self-aware and creative. Thank you. Amen. It is done!"

Archangel Gabriel (God is my strength)

Archangel Gabriel is a remarkable messenger angel who appears in both the Old and New Testaments of the Holy Bible, although he is not directly referred to as an archangel. Known as the angel of revelation and annunciation, Archangel Gabriel can help us to achieve clarity and purity of mind by revealing divine truth and intuitive understanding within our consciousness. Universally he is recognized as a very important divine messenger of God, especially as he announces the planned births of John the Baptist and Jesus Christ. This magnificent archangel can help us to communicate the divine light expression of our soul in a harmonious and pure manner. Archangel Gabriel is intimately connected to harmonizing the divine feminine within all souls, and his divine light frequency also assists all those who desire help with conception, pregnancy, and the welfare of children.

Divine Light Message

"The importance of grounding your energy is one of protection, clarity, and vitality. When you are fully grounded in the present moment, you are more vital, alert, and creative, and you have greater clarity of mind. When you allow your energies to be scattered through being stuck in the pain of the past, or by unnecessarily worrying ahead of yourself in the future, then you naturally become quickly unbalanced. Scattered energies affect your mindfulness, which can then cause daily discord, strife, and the inability to concentrate. If this lack of mindfulness continues, there is more chance to literally lose body balance such that you find mishaps, accidents, and clumsiness become more likely. This significant grounding prayer will help to bring your focus back into the present moment to anchor your soul's light through body awareness and through your connection to the physical realm, so you can regain your vital power and improve your self-awareness. Grounding your energies is so beneficial to you that it also helps to create greater harmony between the physical and the spiritual realms of light, therefore helping you in your cocreative and manifesting abilities. You can also help to ground your energies through your mindful connection with nature, and through breathing and body-awareness exercises. It is time to take greater responsibility for your self-awareness so that your human soul can move onto experiencing new levels of light and creativity that will bring you greater fulfillment, vitality, and radiant joy."

Government of Light Prayer with Archangel Michael
(To send divine light to help positively influence the world's leaders)

"Archangel Michael, please light up the combined consciousness of all of the world's governments and leaders with God's royal blue divine light

*frequency of His perfect truth and protection. Let
the power of the light invoke and awaken the
universal truth of harmony, unity, and oneness
in all who are ready to listen and lead for the
greatest good of humanity. Thank you. Amen. It is
done!"*

Archangel Michael (He who is like God)

Archangel Michael is probably the most famous and
universally known archangel of them all. His magnificent celestial body is the divine expression of God's
power, absolute truth, and protection. He is depicted
in great works of art as a mighty angelic being who
carries a protective shield and powerful sword of light,
often referred to as the "sword of truth." Some have
called him a warrior angel because of the biblical reference to his casting down the fallen angel, Lucifer.
Archangel Michael can help us to slay the fears of our
shadow nature, to break through our illusionary limitations with the power of God's truth, and to overcome
our weaknesses with divine courage and fortitude.
The divine light power bestowed on this astonishing
archangel by God is truly remarkable. When we reach
out to him for help, he will instantly intervene and
guide us through our most ardent struggles, and will
divinely protect us in all our ways.

Divine Light Message

"Through this important, influential prayer, the
royal blue divine light frequency will help to
awaken divine truth within the individual and
combined consciousness of government officials
and world leaders, for the greatest good and

continued evolution of humanity. We angels have observed how many of your governments often make decisions that do not have a firm spiritual foundation as an enlightened base for the good of the whole. They are more materially focused on gaining increased power and greed based on their illusionary fear, perceived separation from one another, and their lack of provision. Some governments are less spiritually evolved than others as they do not consider the pain and terror they inflict upon their nation and upon other nations of the world. All nations' actions greatly impact one another: spiritually, karmically, and physically. Destructive choices bring unnecessary suffering and death that also accounts for world fear, war, and famine. Your prayer of light is greatly received and will be used to bring illumination of God's truth to those who are happy to receive the vibration and reawaken. Light intelligence can only influence those human souls who are ready and willing to listen because you live in a world where God has given man the free-will power to create his own actions. Your prayer will continuously help us angels of light to influence truth where it is most needed until the time comes when man willfully chooses the path of light over that of destruction. Thank you for your light blessing; you are truly helping us to anchor the light of truth within the world to make a positive global difference."

Heartbreak Healing Prayer with Archangel Chamuel
(To help you overcome romantic heartbreak)

"Archangel Chamuel, please light up my broken heart and soul with God's rose pink divine light frequency of His perfect love. I allow the light to help comfort and support me during this difficult time. I willingly release my tears, sadness, and loneliness to the light to be dissolved and replaced with divine love. Please help me to forgive where necessary, so we can both move on without any resentment and have energetic closure. I know that with your loving support I will soon heal through the journey of my heartbreak and live to love again. Thank you. Amen. It is done!"

Archangel Chamuel (He who sees God/He who seeks God)

Archangel Chamuel is an astonishingly radiant angel who is the beautiful embodiment of God's all-powerful divine love. His remarkable angelic service is to continuously out-ray God's divine love to all of humanity to help us overcome and rise above the illusionary fear of worldly appearances and false judgments. Divine love is at the origin of our being, and Archangel Chamuel inspires us to recognize and observe the divinity within ourselves and within all souls, and to express unconditional love for our self and others. Divine love is the most powerful cosmic force within the universe that can help to awaken us to the oneness and unity of creation, so that what we personally create is beneficial for the whole. It is the spectacular light that enables us to evolve our human souls to experience greater dimensions of light and consciousness.

Divine Light Message

"Allow this moment to be one of deep surrender into the healing balm of divine love that will help to nurture and comfort you in your time of need. The emotional pain you are experiencing will not endure for as long as you may believe it will, especially when you let our light shine into your heart and soul. You are completely resilient in spirit, and you will overcome the turbulence of heartbreak with a renewed understanding and awareness of your inner self. Romantic heartache is often an inevitable life experience that many souls encounter, and whilst we angels cannot interfere with your experiences, we will truly help you to overcome them and move on from them. The experience you take with you from what you have discovered about yourself within the relationship is what truly counts. Keep hold of the good memories; learn from the not-so-good; forgive where necessary; and know and believe that love can and will reenter your life when the healing light of time has brought resolution within your heart. Believe that we are with you and are offering celestial comfort to soothe your heart and soul. Life is precarious at times, but nonetheless it is precious and is everlasting. After the initial pain of heartbreak has eased, you may find that you are challenged to keep your heart energy open and trusting. Your emotional pain will attempt to block the light of your heart from allowing love reentry as a misguided form of protection against more suffering. Let the light of your heart blossom and grow into a beautiful rose of love, as the heart that is open and free is the heart that will once again love truly, completely, and unconditionally."

Help Prayer with Your Guardian Angel
(To receive divine assistance from your guardian angel)
"Guardian Angel, please intervene and send me divine help with (be specific and state issue). I willingly release all worry, fear, loneliness, and stress about this situation over to you so that you can take charge and help guide me in God's perfect way. Thank you. Amen. It is done!"

Guardian Angel (Divine Messenger)

God assigned all human souls with their very own guardian angel to help keep watch over them throughout their entire life experience. In the Holy Bible, Jesus makes a reference to the little ones and their angels (Matthew 18:10). All children have guardian angels, and it is these same guardian angels that stay with us throughout the rest of our lives. Guardian angels are always available to help you whenever you encounter any kind of difficulty, trauma, or daily life stress: "For He shall give His angels charge over you to keep you in all your ways" (Psalm 91:11). They are closely aligned with our consciousness because they have been with us from the moment we are born. They know the exact stage of our spiritual growth and what our soul's purpose is for this incarnation. Their most important task is to help us reawaken the divine knowledge and power of God within us so that we can consciously participate in our soul's evolution. They take our prayers to God through the intervention of the archangels, and they bring back the answers we require in harmony with our soul's plan. Guardian angels intervene in our lives in many different and wonderful ways: They influence our consciousness with words of divine inspiration. They intuitively nudge us to meet with the right people, experts, and opportunities along our life path. They send divine light to help us heal when we are sick, suffering, and low on vitality. And they work behind the scenes of our life to divinely protect us from any harmful intentions, both seen and unseen. They often save us from such without us ever knowing. Guardian angels truly are a divine gift to our human soul sent from God because we are so dearly treasured.

Divine Light Message

"Beautiful soul, your prayer for divine assistance is being dealt with as you read these inspired words. Divine love flows through me to always serve you in accordance with the light of your soul's plan and evolution. I am with you spiritually in all that you do. My love for you is unconditional and nonjudgmental, as you mature your soul's light through various daily life experiences. I do what I can to gently steer you toward making the wisest choices in your times of need, without ever taking away any of your free-will power to choose and create life experiences for yourself. I rejoice at your soul's deep desire to reawaken to ever greater levels of consciousness, and I nudge you in the right direction for you to do so. You can ask me to intercede with anything in your life, and I will gladly assist in the spirit of divine love and harmony for the good of the whole. Whether you desire help in obtaining a new job, rediscovering peace in your heart, or to find true love—I will be there for you. If you need healing or comfort, I will be there. Allow me to chase away your fears and to bring your consciousness to a beautiful place of peace and understanding. Divine help is on hand for you right now. Keep your hope and faith strong and know that you are being divinely guided, blessed and watched over. Surrender your impatience to God, and you will soon observe wonderful new opportunities arising."

Holy Spirit Prayer
(To receive divine protection and supernatural power from the Holy Spirit)

"I ask for the white light of the Holy Spirit to surround and protect me in all my ways. I ask for the white light of the Holy Spirit to comfort me in my times of need. I ask for the white light of the Holy Spirit to breathe new life into (state life area you require help in) for my greatest good. I willingly choose to acknowledge that the Holy Spirit of God is alive within me and that I Am a brilliant divine light of God. Thank you, God. Amen. It is done!"

The Holy Spirit

The Holy Spirit is the supernatural force of God's light that exists within every human soul. This remarkable divine power is available to help us at all times. The presence of God's power that is the living light of the Holy Spirit can greatly comfort us in our time of need and protect us from all harm. The Holy Spirit can strengthen our soul's light to help us overcome life's adversities and struggles, it can help us to heal when we are sick and suffering, and it can breathe new life into situations that we feel are hopeless. This miraculous light directly emanates from the One primordial light of Creation to breathe the breath of God's essence into all of existence. It is what infuses each human soul with the spark and spirit of God so that they always have the light of Source within them to help navigate their way home. The Holy Spirit can help to awaken us to our noble divine heritage by bringing to light divine truth and revealing more of our soul's evolutionary path.

Divine Light Message

"The Holy Spirit is the spectacular fire of God's spirit and love within you that is the radiant essence of your soul's light. When you pray the prayer of the Holy Spirit, you ignite a powerful divine force in your body, mind, soul, and life that will bring you many wonderful blessings. The brilliant light of the Holy Spirit is extremely effective in guiding your consciousness to move into greater harmony with unconditional love, divine love, and universal truth. You can physically connect with the divine essence of the Holy Spirit through your own breathing patterns. Take a deep breath in through the nose and exhale slowly out of the mouth as you center your thoughts upon the Holy Spark and presence of God alight within you. This will help to revitalize you, calm your nervous system, harmonize your brain hemispheres, bring you greater clarity of mind, and empower your creativity. The Holy Spirit is your sustenance and will provide you with all of your needs beginning with the very breath of vital life. If it were not for the spark of God within you, then your physical body would lack the vital power it requires to come to life. You can therefore use this miraculous prayer to help you in your hour of need, when you are sick or suffering, and when you need God to breathe new life into a situation that you believe is hopeless. The Holy Spirit of God is your lifeline."

7

*Inner-Child Healing Prayer with
Archangel Gabriel
(To help heal from childhood emotional pain)*
"Archangel Gabriel, please light up the timeline
of my childhood with God's pure white divine
light frequency of His perfect purity, joy, and
vital power. I allow the light to locate and purify
the origin of my emotional pain, traumatic
childhood memories, and unresolved fear, so I
may finally be able to resolve them and release
them. I am willing to forgive where necessary
because I know that this action is for my greatest
good. God's divine purity is now cleansing and
restoring my inner child to bring radiant joy and
vital energy back into the present moment. I
receive this divine healing now in God's perfect
way. Thank you. Amen. It is done!"

Archangel Gabriel (God is my strength)

Archangel Gabriel is a remarkable messenger angel who appears in both the Old and New Testaments of the Holy Bible, although he is not directly referred to as an archangel. Known as the angel of revelation and annunciation, Archangel Gabriel can help us to achieve clarity and purity of mind by revealing divine truth and intuitive understanding within our consciousness. Universally he is recognized as a very important divine messenger of God, especially as he announces the planned births of John the Baptist and Jesus Christ. This magnificent archangel can help us to communicate the divine light expression of our soul in a harmonious and pure manner. Archangel Gabriel is intimately connected to harmonizing the divine feminine within all souls, and his divine light frequency also assists all those who desire help with conception, pregnancy, and the welfare of children.

Divine Light Message

"This inner-child healing prayer can truly help to release you from the emotional pain of your past when you are genuinely ready to let God's light in to help you. There are some unresolved traumatic, fearful, painful, and judgmental issues from your past that you still carry with you today as energetic patterns of dysfunction. These unbalanced patterns can often interfere with the quality of your health and life experiences. Long-term depression, illness, chronic pain, and continuous life struggles can account for many of these unresolved energies. Their destructive root beliefs and limiting perceptions are formed in childhood.

Accepted negative beliefs, and/or the destructive energy of hatred and unforgiveness that you may hold within you due to very difficult and traumatic experiences, can certainly carry many years of unresolved energetic pain into the present moment to negatively impact all aspects of your life. It is time to free yourself from the childhood pain of your past so that you can regain your radiant joy and purity of spirit that is the perfect truth of your soul. Other people's actions and influence may have been severely misguided at times, but do not allow their destructive actions to have any more control over you. All souls exist at different levels of spiritual growth and maturity, and all are learning from their experiences. When you can observe that the light of God is within all, no matter how dim it may be, then you will help to alleviate much of your suffering. The power that is released from this prayer will help to bring you to a greater level of clarity, understanding, forgiveness, and closure. Know that you are always divinely loved and supported."

Note: Each night prior to sleep, visualize yourself being surrounded in pure white light. Imagine it penetrating deep into your body and passing through your bones, muscles, tissues, and into your cells. Know that you are being energetically cleansed by the infusion of the pure white light. Mentally intend that the white light help to heal the unresolved pain of your inner child for your greatest good. If any uncomfortable memories come to the surface to be released, notice them and be willing to let them go without judgment. You will not be given more than you can cope with.

Using this visualization over time, along with saying the powerful divine prayer, will enable you at an inner level to begin energetically processing and resolving your childhood pain.

❧

Insomnia Healing Prayer with Archangel Uriel
(To help you realign with inner peace for sleep)

"Archangel Uriel, please light up my mental energy with the divine power of God's perfect peace. I allow the light to ease my fears, quiet my racing thoughts, and reveal divine solutions to overcome my concerns for my greatest good. I willingly choose to do my part in helping to relax my body and mind prior to sleep. I now release all energetic cause of my insomnia over to the light to be completely resolved and replaced with the inner peace required for deep and lasting sleep. Thank you. Amen. It is done!"

Archangel Uriel (Light of God/Fire of God)

Archangel Uriel is one of the seven archangels of the divine light presence whose important celestial frequency embodies God's divine peace, ministration, and service. This extraordinary angel is personally involved in helping each soul to align with the Christ Light Consciousness alight within their higher-self nature that emanates from the greater universal current. Amplifying the light of God's wisdom within each soul is what ultimately brings the human soul inner peace and spiritual growth through deepened cosmic consciousness. Archangel Uriel is also known as Saint Uriel and is often depicted in art with an open hand holding a flame, which signifies the divine light of God. Other symbolic associations with Archangel Uriel include him carrying a book or scroll, representing divine light knowledge.

Divine Light Message

"The inner battleground of the mind can cause enough energetic disharmony to interfere with deep and lasting sleep. Unconscious fears that are trying to alert you to their presence can often prevent you from entering into the comfort of peaceful sleep. Conscious fears that you are more prominently focused upon can play over and over in your mind, disturbing your sleep. These fears will also seem even more despairing during the early twilight hours. It is natural for you to be able to sleep, and if you are experiencing insomnia that does not positively respond to any relaxation techniques and a commonsense approach, then there is a need for you to face and address whatever is causing your mental energy to stay so alert. The use of medication to help you sleep is a temporary aid that does not reach the true cause of the problem within your consciousness; it just serves to cloud over your mental energy as a form of escape. Also, hoping and wishing for sleep without any intervention on your part will simply keep you stuck in the energetic resistance of insomnia. It is time to ask yourself if you are content with all the elements of your life or if you feel that something important is missing. Are you living in truth and integrity, or do you align with the pangs of guilt? Where inside yourself do you feel you have moved out of balance? The divine light is working to bring harmony where discourse exists, and we angels are gently easing your fears and woes so that you may realign with your soul's inner peace and contentment. The power of prayer can help you to overcome any fear, struggle, and adversity you are presently dealing with that interrupts your sleep. Stop looking only to the material world for answers to your dilemma. It is time to look within and upon the light of a higher power to greatly help you."

Inspiration Prayer with Archangel Jophiel
(To help divinely inspire you)

"Archangel Jophiel, please light up my consciousness with God's golden yellow divine light frequency of His perfect wisdom and inspiration. I allow the light to inspire me with divine intelligence that can help me to create grace, beauty, and love within my life experience. I willingly choose to apply divine inspiration to be a blessing to others and to add my soul's light within the world in accordance with the divine plan. Thank you, Amen. It is done!"

Archangel Jophiel ('Beauty of God)

Archangel Jophiel is a radiant angel of divine light who embodies God's divine wisdom. This remarkable archangel serves to bring enlightenment to humanity to help them awaken to their own higher-self nature and their direct communion with Source energy. Archangel Jophiel's name translates as "beauty of God" because he is able to bring God's thoughts, which always contains the beauty of divine truth, directly into our consciousness to help beautify our mind, body, and soul with divine intelligence. Archangel Jophiel is one of the seven archangels of the divine light presence of God. He is considered as a prince (angel chief) of the law and guardian of divine wisdom by some traditions and is said to be a companion of Archangel Metatron.

Divine Light Message

"This graceful prayer will help to release beautiful inspiration into your creative mind so that you can begin to recreate beauty within your life and in the lives of others. Divine inspiration can flow through you uninterrupted at any time when you participate in centering and stilling your mind, or through the peaceful act of daily meditation. When you align your mind with the higher universal mind of wisdom, then your soul will become illuminated with joyful inspiration. Joy is the natural manifested result of true inspired thought. Inspiration will awaken your soul to cocreate light, truth, and beauty that is greatly fulfilling for you, and also for the one who admires and is gladly blessed by your creation. The love of your soul's essence is imparted within all of your inspired actions and creations, and others can feel the depth of the light that is contained within them. You become a true inspiration to others when you express the truth and beauty of your soul through acknowledging the guidance of your heart without fear. Your grand example will help to awaken inspiration within their own heart and soul to do the same. Divine inspiration is revealing new ideas of beauty to you now. Take these inspired thoughts as seeds of light that can grow into a beautiful rainbow of magnificence with your extra tender care and your willful actions. We angels of light are joyful messengers of God's inspiration, so open your heart to us that we may continuously inspire you."

J

Joy Alignment Prayer with Archangel Gabriel
(To help you amplify the radiant joy of your soul)

"Archangel Gabriel, please light up the radiant joy of my soul's light with God's pure white divine light frequency of His perfect purity and joy. I allow the light to instruct my consciousness in my return to the true joy of my spirit. The white light is purifying all disappointments and illusionary beliefs that shadow my light and cause me to temporarily forget my true radiance. I willingly choose to align my heart and soul with the joy within me so I may experience, create, and attract true joyful experiences in my life. Thank you. Amen. It is done!"

Archangel Gabriel (God is my strength)

Archangel Gabriel is a remarkable messenger angel who appears in both the Old and New Testaments of the Holy Bible, although he is not directly referred to as an archangel. Known as the angel of revelation and annunciation, Archangel Gabriel can help us to achieve clarity and purity of mind by revealing divine truth and intuitive understanding within our consciousness. Universally he is recognized as a very important divine messenger of God, especially as he announces the planned births of John the Baptist and Jesus Christ. This magnificent archangel can help us to communicate the divine light expression of our soul in a harmonious and pure manner. Archangel Gabriel is intimately connected to harmonizing the divine feminine within all souls, and his divine light frequency also assists all those who desire help with conception, pregnancy, and the welfare of children.

Divine Light Message

"Joy originates from the dazzling radiant light of your soul's divine spark. Therefore, you do not need to seek the feeling of joy elsewhere as it is already alight within you; it just needs to be amplified. Joyful experiences simply add more joy to the light of joy that is you, which can help you to glimpse your true self. At this time an aspect of your consciousness is seeking to discover the path of greater joy. This joyfulness-boosting prayer will instruct your consciousness in your graceful return to the true radiant joy of your spirit. Radiant joy creates an energy frequency so powerful that the light it emits can heal illness, relieve chronic pain, overcome depression, and inspire longevity. You have probably heard that laughter is the best medicine; this is because it positively alters the chemistry of your physiology. True radiant joy is even more powerful than laughter for it radiates inner peace, truth, love, and vitality throughout your entire being. Positivity, laughter, and happiness are wonderful side effects of true radiant joy. Over time, life's hurdles and disappointments often diminish the light of your radiant joy and it can become harder to remember the natural joy that you are. There is a pull to look elsewhere for joyful experiences instead of focusing on the light within you. This prayer will help you to refocus in the correct direction so you begin to amplify your soul's radiant joy. You will then feel, express, create, and attract more joyful life experiences."

Judgment/Criticism Healing Prayer with Archangel Chamuel (To help you dissolve critical and judgmental thoughts)

"Archangel Chamuel, please light up my heart's energy with God's rose pink divine light frequency of His perfect love. I allow the light to help dissolve my critical and judgmental shadow nature and to bring me back into harmonious balance with divine love. I willingly choose to open my heart energy to perceive the divine spark and light of God within myself and all others. I now release all need to harshly judge and criticize myself and others. Thank you. Amen. It is done!"

Archangel Chamuel (He who sees God/He who seeks God)

Archangel Chamuel is an astonishingly radiant angel who is the beautiful embodiment of God's all-powerful divine love. His remarkable angelic service is to continuously out-ray God's divine love to all of humanity to help us overcome and rise above the illusionary fear of worldly appearances and false judgments. Divine love is at the origin of our being, and Archangel Chamuel inspires us to recognize and observe the divinity within ourselves and within all souls, and to express unconditional love for our self and others. Divine love is the most powerful cosmic force within the universe that can help to awaken us to the oneness and unity of creation, so that what we personally create is beneficial for the whole. It is the spectacular light that enables us to evolve our human souls to experience greater dimensions of light and consciousness.

Divine Light Message

"Judging and criticizing yourself and others creates limitations of light within your mind, body, and soul expression. When you criticize and judge others or when others criticize and judge you, it is from a place of ignorance where misconceived perceptions shadow the truth of the soul's pure origin. We angels help you to align with the unconditional light of your higher self, where no judgmental attitudes exist. Your shadow nature is where judgments and criticisms thrive until you allow the light of your higher self to shine through and dissolve them. When you are in a situation where you will have the choice to judge and criticize others, we angels will gently whisper words of light so you can willfully choose unconditional love to walk upon higher ground. All human souls travel on the path of soul perfection, and this diversity of light levels within the world can often cause elitism and righteousness to prevail amongst those who feel they know best. What you judge and criticize in another is also an important energetic clue to what shadow aspect you still need to eliminate within yourself. Another person's light frequency is a clever energetic mirror for you to perceive the quality of your own soul's light. Allowing the unconditional love of your higher self more illumination in your life will enable you to perceive and accept others and yourself in a whole new light."

Karmic Healing Prayer with Archangel Zadkiel
(To help clear, resolve, and rebalance karma)

"Archangel Zadkiel, please light up my karmic timelines with God's violet flame of His perfect transformation, transmutation, and freedom. I allow the light to help me transmute all karmic ties that have served their purpose, to bring greater creative freedom to my soul. I willingly choose to resolve any karma that is brought to my awareness and to rebalance it for my greatest good. I am ready to evolve my soul's light in harmony with the divine plan of creation. Thank you. Amen. It is done!"

Archangel Zadkiel (Righteousness of God)

Archangel Zadkiel is an extraordinary celestial angel who embodies the divine light frequency of the all-powerful violet flame and is said to be one of the seven archangels of the divine light presence of God. The divine power of God encoded within the violet flame is truly miraculous. He is known as the archangel of God's benevolence, mercy, and memory, therefore indicating his specialized ability to locate destructive cellular memories within our timelines so they can be immediately resolved and transmuted. Archangel Zadkiel's divine light emanates with the righteousness of God, helping us to correct and transform old patterns of restrictive and destructive energies whether they be rooted in our ancestral timeline, this timeline, or from our own soul's timeline. The violet light can help to resolve and release karmic ties and other negative attachments that interfere with a person's health, vitality, and spiritual well-being.

Divine Light Message

"Divine clemency is yours through this practical karmic healing prayer. You have reached a significant level of light vibration within your consciousness that entitles you to karmic dispensation of old discordant energies. These stagnant karmic residues have served their purpose and can now be transformed to bring your soul into greater harmony with divine love. This is exciting news as a large amount of limiting karma can instantly be dissolved and resolved in accordance with your higher self, to help free you from prior physical and spiritual burdens. God's miraculous violet light will shine through all timelines and free you from the energetic ties and resistance that have weakened the full power of your soul's brilliance. You will naturally amplify your creative potential so that you can light up your life with greater divine splendor. You are continuously evolving your soul through undoing many errors in consciousness that have created countless limitations of your light and power. As you begin to increase this light quotient within your soul, you will naturally ascend in vibrational frequency to experience a whole new level of creativity. Keep clearing old and limiting beliefs from your consciousness so that you can bring more of your higher-self nature into your daily life experience. When you hold enough light within your soul, you will transform your consciousness to such a degree that karma will no longer be part of your dimensional experience."

Knowledge/Study Prayer with Archangel Jophiel
(To help illuminate and support your path of study)

"Archangel Jophiel, please light up my consciousness with God's golden yellow divine light frequency of His perfect wisdom and inspiration. I allow the light to inspire and support me in my chosen area of study. I am open to receiving divine wisdom to help guide me in my path of spiritual enlightenment. I willingly choose to share the experience of my developed

knowledge, gift, talent, and light with others to add beauty and blessings to their life, and to add deeper meaning and fulfillment to my own. Thank you. Amen. It is done!"

Archangel Jophiel (Beauty of God)

Archangel Jophiel is a radiant angel of divine light who embodies God's divine wisdom. This remarkable archangel serves to bring enlightenment to humanity to help them awaken to their own higher-self nature and their direct communion with Source energy. Archangel Jophiel's name translates as "beauty of God" because he is able to bring God's thoughts, which always contains the beauty of divine truth, directly into our consciousness to help beautify our mind, body, and soul with divine intelligence. Archangel Jophiel is one of the seven archangels of the divine light presence of God. He is considered as a prince (angel chief) of the law and guardian of divine wisdom by some traditions and is said to be a companion of Archangel Metatron.

Divine Light Message

"You are being spiritually supported in your path of study and enlightenment. Whether you are taking exams, learning a new skill, developing a unique talent, or researching information, a higher power will join forces with you and illuminate your consciousness with divine intelligence and guidance. Through the use of this supportive prayer, we angels can help you to concentrate, and absorb and retain new knowledge so that you can perfectly integrate your study into your life to bring you the wisdom of experiencing what you know. Study will provide you with new opportunities to serve, be fulfilled, and succeed within the physical realm through the blessings of creative service you can offer others, and from a natural increase of abundance to meet your material life needs. Abundance arises from the patient development of your personal skill or life talent so that the seeds of your study will eventually blossom into fruit. It is a natural desire of your human soul to learn new knowledge and to experience new levels of creativity that will lead you to greater heights of fulfillment. You have so much wisdom within you that is yet untapped, and your path to spiritual enlightenment is the path of study that will enable you to tap into this grand version of your wise, divine self. We angels have heard your prayer for help as you move toward learning more knowledge in the material world that will continuously serve you throughout your life. We will help you to retain that knowledge within your soul's light and to be able to call upon it whenever it is needed."

L

Leadership Prayer with Archangel Metatron
(To help you develop leadership qualities)
"Archangel Metatron, please light up my mind,
body, and soul with divine intelligence to help me
develop strong leadership skills and qualities.
I allow the light to help correct any limitations
in my character that will interfere with my
responsibility of leadership for the greatest good
of the whole. I willingly choose to open my heart's
energy to lead others in compassion and integrity,
and to stay true to the guidance of my higher self.
Thank you. Amen. It is done!"

Archangel Metatron

Archangel Metatron maintains celestial charge over the brilliant light source in the heavenly cosmos where his face is said to be more dazzling than the sun. He is known by some sources as the chancellor of heaven who also serves as a celestial scribe. This astonishingly powerful angel is considered to be amongst the highest of the angels and is the embodiment of ancient knowledge and cosmic wisdom. Archangel Metatron is said to have been the prophet Enoch, the great grand-father of the biblical Noah, who through his spiritual enlightenment was then transformed into an angel upon his bodily ascension into heaven. He is associated as the co-brother of the Archangel Sandalphon due to their similar human-soul-to-angelic-light ascension status. Archangel Metatron is thought to perfectly understand the sacred geometric design of the cosmos and is an expert of soul ascension and light-body integration work.

Divine Light Message

"As you move into this period of leadership, there will be many times when you will have to assert your authority as a leader to give clear direction, inspiration, and knowledge to others. This divine prayer will help to support you in your role and will awaken you to the deeper spiritual qualities of truth, love, and integrity that will make you into a great leader. There will be times when you may begin to doubt your ability to lead due to the extra responsibility placed on your shoulders, but truly know that you are fully equipped in the sight of God. Sometimes difficult decisions are required of your position, but when these are made with love, compassion, and a higher intuitive under-standing, then these decisions will always work out for the greatest good of the whole. You are a true blessing in your service to others when you lead with your heart's energy fully empow-ered. When you become more confident of your leadership role, and if you desire to expand your leadership qualities, then we angels will help to take you further through developing the divine attributes of excellence and dedication to universal service. Divine light will only help to expand the power of your earthly influence when what you offer through leadership skills is in perfect harmony with the universal truth of divine love, peace, and unity."

Life Purpose Prayer with Archangel Michael
(To help you align with your life's plan and activate your soul's talents)

"Archangel Michael, please light up my consciousness with God's royal blue divine light frequency of His perfect truth. I allow the light to reveal to me the truth of my soul's talents, abilities, and skills that can become an integral part of my life's purpose. I willingly choose to develop and utilize my soul's talents for the greatest good of myself and the whole. Thank you. Amen. It is done!"

Archangel Michael (He who is like God)

Archangel Michael is probably the most famous and universally known archangel of them all. His magnificent celestial body is the divine expression of God's power, absolute truth, and protection. He is depicted in great works of art as a mighty angelic being who carries a protective shield and powerful sword of light, often referred to as the "sword of truth." Some have called him a warrior angel because of the biblical reference to his casting down the fallen angel, Lucifer. Archangel Michael can help us to slay the fears of our shadow nature, to break through our illusionary limitations with the power of God's truth, and to overcome our weaknesses with divine courage and fortitude. The divine light power bestowed on this astonishing archangel by God is truly remarkable. When we reach out to him for help, he will instantly intervene and guide us through our most ardent struggles, and will divinely protect us in all our ways.

Divine Light Message

"You have often asked and contemplated what your life purpose is without realizing that your true life purpose is to live as consciously as you can with an awareness of your own soul's light and origin. You are here to create divine love and truth on earth in harmony with the good of the whole, in a way that perfectly suits your conscious nature. You already have astonishing soul talents and creative skills that are a natural aspect of your consciousness that can be brought out into the light of your awareness, developed, and utilized at any time you desire to be more actively creative. Shine the light of unconditional love in thought, word, and action, and you are truly participating in your life's purpose that will bring you to experience greater fulfillment and joy. Soul evolution is your life purpose; however at the material-life level, you desire to be appointed to some significant role that you can associate to your life purpose. You witness the talents of others and you perceive that they are specifically born to do that kind of life work. What they have done is to follow through on their heart's desire, carried deep within their spiritual DNA, to develop and physically express their light in a way that perfectly suits them. If they took no willful action to nourish the heartfelt desire they were born with, then it would not become a physical aspect of their life's purpose. So while you are born with certain gifts, talents, and heartfelt desires encoded within your spiritual DNA, they often remain stagnant until you activate them with creative intention and power. If you have no desire to actively do or be anything, or you falsely believe that you have no life purpose, then you not only miss the true point of life, but you also temporarily block divine creative inspiration flowing through your higher self and spiritual DNA into your consciousness to help you live your life at your greatest potential. Through stating this prayer, along with your added faith and a desire to serve/express your light, you will help to activate your soul's innate talents that will enable you to have a deep and fulfilling life purpose."

Loneliness Prayer with Archangel Chamuel
(To help you overcome loneliness)
"Archangel Chamuel, please light my heart and
soul with God's rose pink divine light frequency

of His perfect love. I allow the light to help ease
the emotional pain of my loneliness and to bring
my consciousness to a place of harmony and
unity with Source. I willingly choose to open my
heart to give and receive love and companionship
without condition. Please guide me to meet with
the right people and opportunities that can bring
more joy and fulfillment into my life. Thank you.
Amen. It is done!"

Archangel Chamuel (He who sees God/He who seeks God)

Archangel Chamuel is an astonishingly radiant
angel who is the beautiful embodiment of God's all-
powerful divine love. His remarkable angelic service
is to continuously out-ray God's divine love to all of
humanity to help us overcome and rise above the illusionary fear of worldly appearances and false judgments. Divine love is at the origin of our being, and
Archangel Chamuel inspires us to recognize and
observe the divinity within ourselves and within all
souls, and to express unconditional love for our self
and others. Divine love is the most powerful cosmic
force within the universe that can help to awaken us
to the oneness and unity of creation, so that what we
personally create is beneficial for the whole. It is the
spectacular light that enables us to evolve our human
souls to experience greater dimensions of light and
consciousness.

Divine Light Message

"Your feelings of loneliness and abandonment do not need to continue for any longer in your life experience if you are willing to release them over to the light. For in truth it is impossible for you to be truly alone, as you have a guardian angel to bring spiritual comfort and support to you in times of need, and many unseen friends and angels that unconditionally love you, who draw close by your light. You will always have this special companionship within the light. Feelings of loneliness can often stem from a false belief that you are separate from God and others. This limiting belief can interfere in your ability to find and form lasting companionship. Other limiting beliefs involving your self-worth and your deservedness to be happy, can also cause frustration and unnecessary experiences of loneliness within your life. We angels have heard your desire to overcome your loneliness and to create a more rewarding, varied, and joyful daily life. Through the use of this loving prayer, we will help to bring your consciousness to a place of truth and light. Blessings of new friendships and new opportunities will soon present themselves for your greater fulfillment. Do what you can to help yourself with these new beginnings so that you do not close the door on your heart's desire for companionship. Overcome any shyness in your soul and any limiting belief by examining them in the light of divine truth, which holds you as a magnificent being of love and light that is always connected to Source."

Love (Soul Mate) Prayer with Archangel Haniel (To help you attract true love)

"Archangel Haniel, please light my consciousness and life experience with God's glorious divine love. I allow the light to expand my heart's energy to help me attract true love into my life that is a perfect vibrational match for my soul. I willingly choose to resolve old patterns of romantic pain that you bring to my awareness so that I can be free to give and receive love without sabotaging interference and fear of loss. I am ready to commit to the experience of true love with peace, unity, and sincerity. Thank you. Amen. It is done!"

Archangel Haniel (Grace of God)

Archangel Haniel is the divine embodiment of God's grace, love, and joy. A beautiful rose gold light is associated with his divine light frequency. In some researched sources, Archangel Haniel is said to have transported the prophet Enoch into heaven before Enoch became the Archangel Metatron. This graceful archangel is aligned to the energy frequency of the planet Venus, also symbolically known as the planet of love, or the Star of Love. He can personally help to awaken romantic love within us and bring harmony, joy, and romance back into relationships that are faltering. He also helps us to harmonize our relationship with divine love and delivers God's grace to us through our intuitive nature. You can ask Archangel Haniel to help you develop a greater intuitive awareness due to his remarkable sensitivity and understanding.

Divine Light Message

"Love is the most powerful force in the universe. It is the creative, protective force that is imbued within all of creation and is what unifies all as One. When you pray the prayer of love, you are asking the Divine to bring into your reality the vibrational force that matches your own in true love. Soul-mate love can therefore be expressed as a perfect match for your consciousness. It is far greater than only that of physical chemistry and sexual desire. It also harmonizes in spiritual unity, emotional support, lasting friendship, and engaging mental depth—thereby creating genuine compatibility of the mind, body, and soul. True soul-mate love is born from the pure desire to connect on all levels with a soul in honesty and integrity, while giving them and yourself the freedom to express the uniqueness of your light within the world. Soul-mate love is faithful, sincere, kind, and strong, and the pure energetic effects of this union will last for all eternity, no matter how long the physical relationship itself survived. It is therefore possible for there to be more than one experience of finding true love in your lifetime, as time brings change and with it new paths. As love is eternal, nothing special is ever lost from your previous soul-love connection, and all is understood in the light of higher perception within the heaven realms. We angels are created out of pure divine love, just as you are, and nothing makes us more joyful than witnessing the delightful new beginnings of pure love between two soul mates coming together as one. As you pray this prayer of love, we will help you to activate your heart's desire to attract true soul-mate love to you."

M

*Manifesting Prayer with Archangel Raziel
(To help you manifest your deepest dreams and
heartfelt desires)*

*"Archangel Raziel, please light up my divine
creative spark with God's magnificent divine
intelligence and creative power. I allow the light
to help sculpt and empower my manifesting
abilities, and to help me resolve any disturbances
in the full expression of my soul's light. I willingly
choose to use my creative power in harmony with
divine truth and divine love so that I can manifest
beauty and joy for the greatest good of myself
and others. Thank you. Amen. It is done!"*

Archangel Raziel (Secret of God)

This marvelous archangel is the legendary subject
of the Book of the Angel Raziel, which is said to contain secret knowledge. He is imbued with remarkable
divine wisdom and is the keeper of knowledge, mysteries of the world, and the secrets of God. His divine

light frequency embodies all seven rays of divine light combined as one extraordinary light emanation signifying the rainbow ray. The divine light intelligence of the rainbow ray can reveal to us the divine knowledge we require to help us navigate our human soul through our physical incarnation in harmony with our life's plan. Archangel Raziel can help to illuminate our spiritual journey back into the realms of light and God consciousness.

Divine Light Message

"As a divine light being, you already have the extraordinary creative power within you to manifest into reality that which you need and desire. This is the glory of your own divine authority that invokes spiritual power within your spoken word, sincere intention, imagined outcome, and actions. The divine spark of God is eternally alight within you as you are simply a smaller divine part of a greater divine whole. This spiritual understanding immediately illuminates and strengthens your manifesting power as your own God consciousness moves into perfect harmony with the greater universal Source. As a permanent aspect of Source, you can ask this greater divine intelligence and benevolent power for spiritual assistance at any time to help empower your soul's creative light to manifest, create, and attract your deepest dreams and heartfelt desires. Belief and faith in your own divine light to create joy and beauty within your life and the lives of others will help to activate and release powerful spiritual assistance for God's grace to enter into your life.

Divine intelligence knows exactly how to help you amplify your creative power and will bring you the insight and guidance that is required to do so. If there is no real desire to grow in spiritual wisdom, then this will interfere with your manifesting results. There really is nothing that you can't achieve or manifest if it is in harmony with divine love. You truly have the power within you to create and manifest great abundance, vital health, and fulfillment. You are a powerful, limitless being with untapped creative potential, so take back your power today and start creating a grand, rewarding, and joyful life experience."

Marriage/Relationship Healing Prayer with Archangel Haniel
(To help bless your marriage in divine love)

"Archangel Haniel, please light up my marriage union and vows with God's perfect divine love for the greatest good of us both. I allow the light to help bring harmony back into our relationship to reunite us together as one in beauty, grace, sincerity, and joy. I willingly choose to love and respect my partner without conditions. I ask for a divine blessing to be placed on our marriage today so that it can be restored and strengthened in the light of God's perfect divine love. Thank you. Amen. It is done!"

Archangel Haniel (Grace of God)

Archangel Haniel is the divine embodiment of God's grace, love, and joy. A beautiful rose gold light is associated with his divine light frequency. In some researched sources, Archangel Haniel is said to have transported the prophet Enoch into heaven before Enoch became the Archangel Metatron. This graceful archangel is aligned to the energy frequency of the planet Venus, also symbolically known as the planet of love, or the Star of Love. He can personally help to awaken romantic love within us and bring harmony, joy, and romance back into relationships that are faltering. He also helps us to harmonize our relationship with divine love and delivers God's grace to us through our intuitive nature. You can ask Archangel Haniel to help you develop a greater intuitive awareness due to his remarkable sensitivity and understanding.

Divine Light Message

"Marriage is a beautiful union of light held between both souls that brings with it many unique lessons and opportunities for spiritual growth. Unconditional love is the strongest attribute of a marriage union where each soul loves and accepts the other with all of their weaknesses and shadows. There are times of strength and times of vulnerability within the journey of a marriage, and it is this unfaltering, unconditional love that is able to help you forgive, forget, and see the trying times through. We angels have heard your heartfelt prayer for our divine intervention in the light union of your marriage, and we are bringing light to the parts that have dimmed. If both of you hold true to the light of your spiritual union within your heart and soul, then anything can be overcome within the marriage and it can be completely restored. If you feel that your marriage vows have no more life left within them, then you will be surprised at what a sincere heartfelt prayer, said for the greatest good of you both, can do. The light of God can breathe new life back into the union of a marriage when all seems lost. We angels are helping you both to recognize the wonderful blessings within your shared partnership, and through this prayer, we are sending you a divine blessing of love to help empower your soul connection. We will help to awaken divine understanding and compassion within each of you, so that you may both work together in harmony and light to help heal the relationship imbalance."

Miracle Affirmation Prayer with the Christ Light Consciousness (To help you align with the source of divine miracles)

"The Christ Light Consciousness is perfectly expressing a divine miracle in me, through me, and around me now. I am willing to receive a divine miracle now for (state desired miracle), for my greatest and highest good. Thank you, God. Amen. It is done!"

The Christ Light Consciousness

The Christ Light Consciousness is the pure divine light intelligence and love that God embodies for the whole of creation that illuminates and radiates throughout the entire universe. The Christ Light Consciousness is also a spectacular aspect of every human soul, no matter what stage of spiritual awakening and maturity they are in, or what religion, if any, they are personally aligned with. The divine aspect that is known as the Christ Light Consciousness is the spark of divine presence that exists within every human soul. It is impossible to be without this God consciousness because our individual souls of light are all birthed from the One primordial ray of God's Divine Light. It is the Light of Lights that weaves us all together in the oneness of Creation. We carry God's consciousness as the higher part of our soul nature to help awaken and illuminate us, to evolve our souls in harmony with divine truth and divine love.

Divine Light Message

"A miracle is a natural progression of heavenly law, and we angels want you to recognize that you live a joyous miracle every day of your life. Miracles surround you and are part of you. When you ask the divine power to work miracles in your life, they are released to you in accordance with your soul's plan and your faith in the light. When all is said and done, and every other avenue of help has been researched, tried, and tested, and "no hope" seems to be the final word, then you need to know that miracles can and will happen for you; these divine acts are freely given to you through the power of your own divine authority to have dominion over all of matter. When you begin to accept that these acts of spiritual greatness are a natural aspect of your true divine nature, then you will come to see that God's favor is already placed upon you and divine miracles are within your reach every moment of your life. The miracle of your glorious divine design (body and soul) is a perfect example of how God's almighty power can create such a miracle of life. Allow your conscious awareness to recognize all the miracles that already exist within your daily life, from the beauty of a flower to the spontaneous healing of ailments and illness with God's grace. When you do this, you quickly align your light with the faith and belief that life is truly miraculous, and therefore miracles can be a true reality for you now."

Motivation Prayer with Archangel Michael (To help you become motivated)

"Archangel Michael, please light up my mind, body, and soul with God's royal blue divine light frequency of His perfect truth, power, and courage. I allow the light to help motivate my free-will power and to give me the spiritual strength and courage I require to succeed on my life's path. I willingly choose to take positive creative action in my daily life to overcome any stagnation of my soul's expression, and light up my life with unlimited potential. Thank you. Amen. It is done!"

Archangel Michael (He who is like God)

Archangel Michael is probably the most famous and universally known archangel of them all. His magnificent celestial body is the divine expression of God's power, absolute truth, and protection. He is depicted in great works of art as a mighty angelic being who carries a protective shield and powerful sword of light, often referred to as the "sword of truth." Some have called him a warrior angel because of the biblical reference to his casting down the fallen angel, Lucifer. Archangel Michael can help us to slay the fears of our shadow nature, to break through our illusionary limitations with the power of God's truth, and to overcome our weaknesses with divine courage and fortitude. The divine light power bestowed on this astonishing archangel by God is truly remarkable. When we reach out to him for help, he will instantly intervene and guide us through our most ardent struggles, and will divinely protect us in all our ways.

Divine Light Message

"At times you may feel despondent, stuck, and irritable, and are therefore unable to motivate yourself into taking any positive action to overcome life's hurdles. Other times you may feel like you have lost your faith in yourself to accomplish your heartfelt desires, and so you lose the inner resolve to strive forward anymore. This motivational prayer will help to empower you with divine strength, courage, and truth to assist you in taking creative steps in faith that will move you forward toward the success and greatness that is rightly yours. We angels are here to motivate you and to give you the spark of energy that you need to light up your own vital fire to overcome those obstacles that keep you tied to your negative feelings. For when you willfully choose to shine your light, you move directly on the creative path toward probable success in all of your endeavors. Divine truth will help to correct the errors in your consciousness that exist, and divine strength will help to ignite the fire of motivation in your heart and your soul so that you may reach for the stars once more. The potential for greatness is always within you; it is the gift the divine creator has given to every human soul. Think of your previous pressures, struggles, and challenges as helping to reveal the tremendous creative light of your true divine self. When you are motivated, there is nothing you can't achieve, and we are giving you the energy that you need to fire the rocket of your light into the universe, taking your success to the top of the world. When you are motivated, nothing can hold you back and everything seems possible. It is time to rise to the challenge of the greatness that exists within you. We have heard your prayer and this is our answer—to motivate your motivation. It is done."

Nervous System Prayer with Archangel Jophiel
(To help calm and support your nervous system and relieve stress)

"Archangel Jophiel, please light up my nervous system with God's golden yellow divine light frequency of His perfect divine intelligence. I allow the light to help rebalance the energies of both hemispheres of my brain, to calm my nerves, and to bring me greater clarity of mind. I willingly choose to correct any negative thoughts, beliefs, and habits in the light of divine truth so they are unable to create further nervous tension and stress in my body and mind. Thank you. Amen. It is done!"

Archangel Jophiel (Beauty of God)

Archangel Jophiel is a radiant angel of divine light who embodies God's divine wisdom. This remarkable archangel serves to bring enlightenment to humanity to help them awaken to their own higher-self nature and their direct communion with Source energy. Archangel Jophiel's name translates as "beauty of God" because he is able to bring God's thoughts, which always contains the beauty of divine truth, directly into our consciousness to help beautify our mind, body, and soul with divine intelligence. Archangel Jophiel is one of the seven archangels of the divine light presence of God. He is considered as a prince (angel chief) of the law and guardian of divine wisdom by some traditions and is said to be a companion of Archangel Metatron.

Divine Light Message

"Your body's energies are truly remarkable; they cross over, flow in rhythmic patterns, pulsate, spiral, and spin, and this is just a small example of what they do. For your physical body to stay in a healthy and vital state, your energies follow what divine intelligence has programmed them to do to help support all of the systems and functions of your body. Your glorious nervous system is alight with sensory intelligence, and the energies that support this system naturally cross over between both hemispheres of the brain. However, when there is nervous tension of any kind, then these energies fail to do their task correctly. This is okay as your body has evolved to cope with many different kinds of stress and so it can soon rebalance itself through sleep, exercise, and other means. But when nervous tension is consistent, stress energy builds up and becomes the dominant factor in your energy field, and it becomes harder for your body to energetically rebalance. Frazzled nerves, overreactions, emotional sensitivity, depression, and other physical body ailments are just some of the side effects of this long-term stress response. It is therefore very important to look after your nervous system, and this wonderful healing prayer will invite divine intelligence into your system to help your energies cross over and function optimally. Along with your willful action of doing what you can to correct any negative thoughts, beliefs, and habits, you will soon help to calm your nerves and empower your vitality. It is time for you to free your mental energy of all kinds of stress and pressures that you place on your energetic nervous system. We angels bring you divine illumination to help you gain greater clarity of mind and a life free of excess stress."

Nighttime Prayer with Your Guardian Angel
(To help watch over you, protect you, and guide you during sleep)

"Guardian angel, please divinely protect my body and soul this night and release me from my irrational fears. Send me divine guidance and solutions to my concerns as I enter into a wonderful deep and healing sleep. Thank you. Amen. It is done!"

You can also use this divine affirmation prayer:

"Guardian angel of my light, please protect me now and all through the night. I am grateful for your guidance and love, and the blessings of light from God above."

Guardian Angel (Divine Messenger)

God assigned all human souls with their very own guardian angel to help keep watch over them throughout their entire life experience. In the Holy Bible, Jesus makes a reference to the little ones and their angels (Matthew 18:10). All children have guardian angels and it is these same guardian angels that stay with us throughout the rest of our lives. Guardian angels are always available to help you whenever you encounter any kind of difficulty, trauma, or daily life stress: "For He shall give His angels charge over you to keep you in all your ways" (Psalm 91:11). They are closely aligned with our consciousness because they have been with us from the moment we are born. They know the exact stage of our spiritual growth and what our soul's purpose is for this incarnation. Their most important task is to help us reawaken the divine knowledge and power of God within us so that we can consciously participate in our soul's evolution. They take our prayers to God through the intervention of the archangels, and they bring back the answers we require in harmony with our soul's plan. Guardian angels intervene in our lives in many different and wonderful ways; they influence our consciousness with words of divine inspiration. They intuitively nudge us to meet with the right people, experts, and opportunities along our life path.

They send divine light to help us heal when we are sick, suffering, and low on vitality. And they work behind the scenes of our life to divinely protect us from any harmful intentions both seen and unseen. They often save us from such without us ever knowing. Guardian angels truly are a divine gift to our human soul sent from God because we are so dearly treasured.

Divine Light Message

"Nighttime prayers of protection and guidance will always invite the guardian angels to watch over you and your loved ones as you enter into the evening routine of sleep. The power of prayer, combined with your faith that your prayer has been heard and answered, has a wonderful calming effect on your nervous system that will help you to relax and sleep more peacefully. At nighttime, many of your irrational fears and daily life concerns will often become more prominent because of the peace and quiet, and the lack of physical distraction in your daily life that works to keep your mind busy and away from your issues. These issues attempt to be heard in the quiet time so you can pay attention to them and deal with them accordingly. However, as you try to analyze them and work out solutions to your problems, or you try to ignore them so they keep floating back into your awareness and demand your attention, then your mind's energy can find difficulty in relaxing. If you do manage to fall asleep, then often times nightmares and disturbed patterns of sleep can entail. Your guardian angel is sent by God to help you in all your ways. Surrender all of your fears and concerns to their light, and this will help you to naturally fall asleep. You will also often awake with inspired ideas as solutions to your problems. Your guardian angel protects your body and soul from any discordant energies, both seen and unseen, during your nightly sleep and will surely awake you and intervene if or when necessary for your greatest good. Use this important prayer each night and you will invite a higher power to watch over you."

Obese/Overweight Healing Prayer with Archangel Zadkiel
(To help spiritually support you in releasing excess body weight)

"Archangel Zadkiel, please light up my consciousness with God's violet divine light frequency of His perfect transmutation, transformation, and freedom. I allow the light to locate the origin of my unresolved emotions that interfere with my body's excess weight, and to help me completely resolve and transmute them in God's perfect way. I ask that this healing transformation be brought forward into my present reality to bring freedom to my consciousness to effect physical change. I willingly choose to unconditionally love and accept myself and others with ease and grace. Thank you, God. Amen. It is done!"

Archangel Zadkiel (Righteousness of God)

Archangel Zadkiel is an extraordinary celestial angel who embodies the divine light frequency of the all-powerful violet flame and is said to be one of the seven archangels of the divine light presence of God. The divine power of God encoded within the violet flame is truly miraculous. He is known as the archangel of God's benevolence, mercy, and memory, therefore indicating his specialized ability to locate destructive cellular memories within our timelines so they can be immediately resolved and transmuted. Archangel Zadkiel's divine light emanates with the righteousness of God, helping us to correct and transform old patterns of restrictive and destructive energies whether they be rooted in our ancestral timeline, this timeline, or from our own soul's timeline. The violet light can help to resolve and release karmic ties and other negative attachments that interfere with a person's health, vitality, and spiritual well-being.

Divine Light Message

"This unconditional prayer is centered around resolving any form of energetic imbalance that may be unconsciously participating in keeping your body at a certain size, no matter how strict you are with healthy nutrition and exercise. When body weight issues stubbornly persist when you seem to be doing all the correct and commonsense actions to lose your weight, then it is time to look deeper into your energy fields of resonance. Unresolved emotional issues and sensitivity can also play havoc in your body's size and weight. On top of this, self-criticism, self-hatred, the desire to be perfect—which suggests to your soul that you are not—also unwittingly interferes with your ability to shed any excess weight. This healing prayer will enable you to begin to transmute the origin of any unresolved emotions and to free you of any self-critical, false, and limiting beliefs that do interfere with your body's ability to release its excess weight. We angels will divinely inspire you to help keep your will strong, your consciousness centered in the light of truth, and your heart unconditionally open toward yourself and others. When you free yourself of weighty emotions and you perceive yourself in a whole new light of truth, then you will add tremendous energetic and spiritual support to the healthy lifestyle that you are putting into place. When you learn to love and accept who you truly are, a divine light of God, then this acceptance will illuminate the beauty and vitality of your physical body, whether big or small. The body is a temple for the light of your spirit, and when you come to honor its divine design, one that keeps your heart beating to enable your soul to have a physical life experience, then you will come to empower unconditional love for yourself. It is love and truth that lead you to experience your greatest joy. You are being gently nudged today to realign with your radiant joy."

Obsession Healing Prayer with Archangel Michael (To help you overcome obsession)

"Archangel Michael, please light up my mind, body, and soul with God's royal blue divine light frequency of His perfect truth, strength, and power. I allow the light to join forces with me in overcoming my obsession with (state obsession). I willingly choose to correct all errors in my consciousness by examining them in the light of divine truth and love so that all illusion can dissolve. I now agree to listen to the truth within my heart and soul, and move into greater harmony with my higher self. Thank you. Amen. It is done!"

Archangel Michael (He who is like God)

Archangel Michael is probably the most famous and universally known archangel of them all. His magnificent celestial body is the divine expression of God's power, absolute truth, and protection. He is depicted in great works of art as a mighty angelic being who carries a protective shield and powerful sword of light, often referred to as the "sword of truth." Some have called him a warrior angel because of the biblical reference to his casting down the fallen angel, Lucifer. Archangel Michael can help us to slay the fears of our shadow nature, to break through our illusionary limitations with the power of God's truth, and to overcome our weaknesses with divine courage and fortitude. The divine light power bestowed on this astonishing archangel by God is truly remarkable. When we reach out to him for help, he will instantly intervene and guide us through our most ardent struggles, and will divinely protect us in all our ways.

Divine Light Message

"Any kind of obsession is a clear underlying message to your conscious awareness that you have a certain degree of energetic imbalance somewhere within your spiritual and mental energy fields. In other words, your soul's light is being briefly hindered from its full glorious expression. What is it that you fear about living the truth of your heart and soul? Are you preventing yourself from following through on some special dream that you believe is impossible or too difficult to create? Listening to the truth of your heart and soul will help you to initiate positive subtle changes in the rebalancing of your discordant energies. Any form of obsession is greatly helped through the consistent use of the power of prayer, combined with a clear willful desire to overcome your obsessive nature. This significant divine healing prayer will immediately go to work within your consciousness in accordance with your free-will desire. The spiritual power it evokes can truly help to alleviate much of your struggle with your obsessiveness when you allow the light to join forces with you. Obsessive imbalances have caused you to become focused on an element of your life that does not serve your greatest good and only acts as a temporary delay and interference in the greater expression of your soul's creativity. We angels are helping to rectify these energetic imbalances within you, so you can once more realign with the true joy of your higher self. Love and accept that you have a shadow nature without condemning yourself, as it can easily be overcome with the power of your own divine authority filtering through a strong will to succeed. Your light has dominion over any kind of obsession because when you shine your light on it, you will observe the illusion that has no real power. It is time for you to take back your soul power that has been hindered through the interference of your obsessions. You are ready to move into harmony with divine truth and divine love so that you can rebalance the light of your mind, body, and soul."

P

Peace Prayer with Archangel Uriel
(To help restore your inner peace)

"Archangel Uriel, please light up my mind, body, and soul with the perfect power of God's divine peace. I allow the light to help me resolve discordant energetic issues within me, old and new, that are causing me to lose my inner peace. I willingly choose to think peaceful thoughts, feel peaceful emotions, and to create my own peaceful reality within the world. I am now ready to truly restore my inner peace with ease and grace. Thank you. Amen. It is done!"

Archangel Uriel (Light of God/Fire of God)

Archangel Uriel is one of the seven archangels of the divine light presence whose important celestial frequency embodies God's divine peace, ministration, and service. This extraordinary angel is personally involved in helping each soul to align with the Christ Light Consciousness alight within their higher-self nature that emanates from the greater universal current. Amplifying the light of God's wisdom within each soul is what ultimately brings the human soul inner peace and spiritual growth through deepened cosmic consciousness. Archangel Uriel is also known as Saint Uriel and is often depicted in art with an open hand holding a flame, which signifies the divine light of God. Other symbolic associations with Archangel Uriel include him carrying a book or scroll, representing divine light knowledge.

Divine Light Message

"Peace is a constant light within you and is only dimmed by the shadows of irrational fear and illusion. When you acknowledge the light of truth in your heart and the strength of spirit in your soul, then you will begin to think peaceful thoughts, and inner peace and harmony will soon prevail. This peaceful prayer will help you to resolve old and new issues that keep you from feeling the blessing of inner peace by bringing to your mind where you need to correct any errors in consciousness and by igniting your courage to blast through limiting fears. Resistance to change can also cause lack of peace due to the imagined fears of what could possibly go wrong. You therefore remain in inharmonious situations that you have already lost your peace in due to your unhappiness and soul suppression. Lack of peace within the world also draws your attention to the lack of peace within yourself, and so fear reigns supreme over the light of your inner peace. It is time to allow the presence of peace to express its true nature within you, through you, and around you, so that it permeates within your life and positively influences more peace within the world. Just one person with true peace in their heart and soul will add peaceful energy to the world to help effect peaceful change. Peace is yours to reclaim, and now that you know it has always been within you, never lost, you can begin to restore the inner peace that is rightfully yours. Recognize inner peace as an energy frequency that is not only something born of contentment but is truly an aspect of the Divine Power. The light of divine peace has the ability to transmute the darkness and illusions created by man back into the light of harmony, truth, and unity. Inner peace will soon reveal itself within your conscious awareness; reach out and touch it, for it surrounds you in every minute particle that makes up your reality. Choose your own peaceful reality from now on."

*Prosperity Prayer with Archangel Raphael
(To help you realign with the energy
frequency of prosperity)*
*"Archangel Raphael, please light up my
consciousness with God's emerald green divine
light frequency of His perfect abundance. I
allow the light to help me align my mind with
prosperous thoughts and to rewire inaccurate
beliefs of poverty consciousness and struggle.
I willingly choose to activate the power of my*

*creative expression as I know that God has
already fully equipped me with the power to be
abundant and prosperous. I reclaim my spiritual
power now in thought, word, and action to open
the way for unlimited prosperity to flow into my
life. Thank you. Amen. It is done!"*

Archangel Raphael (God heals)

Archangel Raphael is typically known as God's
divine healing angel who delivers God's all-powerful
healing light to all who call on him for spiritual assistance. Another interpretation of his name is "God
has healed," which suggests that health is already a
firm reality within the mind and sight of God, and
we consistently maintain this reality of perfect health
within our true divine origin. Archangel Raphael's
powerful divine light is therefore administered to help
us to realign with our already-healed and healthy
divine self. His beautiful divine light frequency also
embodies the celestial qualities of divine abundance
and spiritual protection during travel. He holds the
complete wisdom of divine healing science within his
consciousness and is therefore able to help anyone to
develop and tap into their own internal divine healer,
should they desire to understand the deeper truths of
healing.

Divine Light Message

"You have divine prosperity within you; it is a true
aspect of your soul that exists within the creative
light of your spirit. It is the enlightening power
that has dominion over all of matter. This is why

you can recognize God as the real source of your provision because you have the almighty power of God's consciousness alight with divine intelligence within your cells. This divine power, when tapped into, can bring constant nourishment to your life because divine intelligence knows exactly how to create, attract, and manifest prosperous ideas, ventures, situations, and outcomes for your creative comfort and fulfillment. Just like waters nourish the earth, the creative light of your spirit can nourish your life through utilizing the unlimited flow of abundant and prosperous opportunities that are eternally available for any soul who is ready to claim them. Through the active use of this divine prayer, an abundance of opportunities and life experiences will soon provide you with the chance to become more prosperous. This means that along with your faith and belief that God is your provider, you also take creative action to allow the creativity of your God consciousness to work through you. Action is always required on your part as stagnation of action will dry up the ideas and opportunities sent to help you become more prosperous. With each passing day, we angels influence you with prosperous thoughts, giving you the intuitive nudges to help you harness the power of your creative expression in your daily life. In the spiritual realms of light, you are truly already abundant and prosperous, and you just need to allow it to be so in your physical existence."

Psychic Attack Healing Prayer with Archangel Michael
(To help free you from the energetic effects of psychic attack)

"Archangel Michael, please light up my consciousness with God's royal blue divine light frequency of His perfect truth and protection.

I ask that the light immediately free my body, mind, and soul of any destructive energies and harmful intentions sent to me by others, both seen and unseen. I willingly choose to move my thoughts, words, and actions into greater harmony with divine truth and love. I invoke the power of my own divine authority to have dominion over all destructive energies, intentions, and influences. Thank you. Amen. It is done!"

Archangel Michael (He who is like God)

Archangel Michael is probably the most famous and universally known archangel of them all. His magnificent celestial body is the divine expression of God's power, absolute truth, and protection. He is depicted in great works of art as a mighty angelic being who carries a protective shield and powerful sword of light, often referred to as the "sword of truth." Some have called him a warrior angel because of the biblical reference to his casting down the fallen angel, Lucifer. Archangel Michael can help us to slay the fears of our shadow nature, to break through our illusionary limitations with the power of God's truth, and to overcome our weaknesses with divine courage and fortitude.

The divine light power bestowed on this astonishing archangel by God is truly remarkable. When we reach out to him for help, he will instantly intervene and guide us through our most ardent struggles, and will divinely protect us in all our ways.

Divine Light Message
"Psychic attack is energetic attack, and it comes in many forms that can negatively affect the vitality of the body and suppress the creative power of the soul. You already have a powerful auric field to help protect you from unwanted influences, but when you are out of energetic harmony or you are physically unwell, you will naturally weaken the force field of light protection around you. Destructive energetic frequencies can then invade the weakened areas and impact your vibrational space or attach into your energy centers, causing numerous issues. While you are truly capable of ridding yourself of unwanted toxic frequencies through the use of easy energy techniques that help to clear, rebalance, and revitalize your energy field, we angels also acknowledge that sometimes you need our intervention in order to deal with stubborn energetic issues that continuously persist. Working together through prayer and action is even more powerful. When you begin to raise your light levels through moving your consciousness back into greater harmony with divine love in thought, word, and action, then other people's energies will become less bothersome. The power of your prayer now enables us angels to go to work within all of your energy systems and

consciousness to help rid you of toxic influences and attachments that do not serve your soul's light in any suitable way. It is time for you to regain your physical strength and vitality, and to empower your creative spark by taking more active daily care and of your spiritual and energetic anatomy. Know that there is nothing that can spiritually harm you as you already have the divine power and authority bestowed upon you by God to overcome all negativity. This divine authority that dwells deep within your soul is being enhanced by the light of our love and will transmute all low vibrations and empower you."

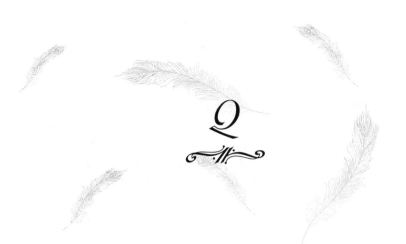

Quarrel Healing Prayer with Archangel Chamuel (To help resolve conflict)

"Archangel Chamuel, please light up my mind, body, and soul with God's rose pink divine light frequency of His perfect love. I allow the light to help me restore peace and harmony in my quarrel with (state name). I willingly choose to open my heart energy and let the light of love dissolve and resolve any blame, guilt, and anger that I am energetically holding about this situation. I send the person (state name) a divine blessing of love and light, and release them to follow their own good. Thank you. Amen. It is done!"

Archangel Chamuel (He who sees God/He who seeks God)

Archangel Chamuel is an astonishingly radiant angel who is the beautiful embodiment of God's all-powerful divine love. His remarkable angelic service

is to continuously out-ray God's divine love to all of humanity to help us overcome and rise above the illusionary fear of worldly appearances and false judgments. Divine love is at the origin of our being, and Archangel Chamuel inspires us to recognize and observe the divinity within ourselves and within all souls, and to express unconditional love for our self and others. Divine love is the most powerful cosmic force within the universe that can help to awaken us to the oneness and unity of creation, so that what we personally create is beneficial for the whole. It is the spectacular light that enables us to evolve our human souls to experience greater dimensions of light and consciousness.

Divine Light Message

"Arguments are a natural aspect of the shadow self, especially when egos have been bruised and judgments fly back and forth. We angels do our best to help all parties perceive others beyond the shadows of the lower nature so that unconditional understanding can bring resolution, and harmony can prevail. It is not necessary to be right in a quarrel, even when you absolutely believe you are right due to other people's immature behaviors. All souls exist at different levels of consciousness, and some are obviously more spiritually mature than others. This understanding can help you to open your heart energy to accept that all human souls are often doing the best they can at the level of light they have consciously attained, and therefore they do not yet know any difference. Do not fall into the habit of spiritual elitism because you may feel you already know better than others as you, and all others, are on a continuous journey to evolve your light expression; there will be plenty of others who are ahead of you as well as behind you. Therefore, the beautiful energy of compassion and spiritual understanding can easily override unnecessary quarrels. Others do have a right to their own beliefs, even when they are not willing to see further than their own limiting assumptions. Trying to force your will upon them to see the light is an interference in their soul's creative expression. When you move out of your wounded shadow nature and you align your mind with the light of higher understanding, then you will bring light into the situation for the greatest good of all. This loving prayer will help to soften your heart and bring light into old and new quarrels so that you can let go of the energetic interference that bonds you in consciousness to reharmonize your souls."

Quantum Healing Prayer with Archangel Metatron
(To help heal and activate the light body)

"Archangel Metatron, please light up my consciousness with God's all-powerful creative light to help realign my multidimensional energies and empower my light body. I allow the light to help me ascend my vibrational frequency to new levels of light and creative power. I willingly *choose to expand my awareness about my magnificent divine design, so I can participate in my own healing and light work for my greatest good. Thank you. Amen. It is done!"*

Archangel Metatron

Archangel Metatron maintains celestial charge over the brilliant light source in the heavenly cosmos where his face is said to be more dazzling than the sun. He is known by some sources as the chancellor of heaven who also serves as a celestial scribe. This astonishingly powerful angel is considered to be amongst the highest of the angels and is the embodiment of ancient knowledge and cosmic wisdom. Archangel Metatron is said to have been the prophet Enoch, the great grandfather of the biblical Noah, who through his spiritual enlightenment was then transformed into an angel upon his bodily ascension into heaven. He is associated as the co-brother of the Archangel Sandalphon due to their similar human-soul-to-angelic-light ascension status. Archangel Metatron is thought to perfectly understand the sacred geometric design of the cosmos and is an expert of soul ascension and light-body integration work.

Divine Light Message

"Quantum healing is multidimensional healing, which includes an understanding of every aspect of your glorious divine design and specialized healing light-work throughout all timelines of existence. You have an exquisite and complicated spiritual and energetic anatomy with powerful magnetic fields of resonance surrounding you.

Your miraculous DNA also has magnetic fields of divine intelligence surrounding each cell, to provide specific instructions to create precise patterns. Within your spiritual DNA, you hold the impressive akashic records of your soul's timeline, the evolutionary history of humanity, divine truth, and a record of everything you have ever accomplished within all timelines of experience that you have partaken. You hold the remarkable totality of your soul's light within you, and you can activate powerful talents and soul abilities that could serve you well in this life when you come into greater alignment and harmony with your multidimensional self. This powerful quantum healing prayer enables you to ignite a specific aspect of your consciousness that is ready to evolve further and expand the creative light source within you. When you allow these subtle energetic changes to take place, you also invite new knowledge and wisdom to enter into your physical life experience to help you understand your exquisite anatomy. With this new understanding, you are able to directly assist your own energetic light source to help you self-heal, increase your vitality, and overcome unnecessary struggle. This important prayer will work in your consciousness in accordance with your spiritual growth so that you can truly begin to contemplate and understand the magnificence of your fantastic divine design. New opportunities will present themselves for you to study and learn from wise spiritual/healing teachers that can support you in your ascension."

Relationship Harmony Prayer with Archangel Uriel
(To help you establish greater harmony within your relationships)

"Archangel Uriel, please light up my heart and soul with God's perfect divine peace. I allow the light to help me restore peace and harmony within my inharmonious relationship with (state person's name). I willingly choose to keep peace in my heart and to perceive (state person's name) in the spiritual light of his/her own splendor. I honor him/her exactly where he/she is in his/her soul's evolution, thereby igniting spiritual peace and harmony in our relationship with each other. Thank you. Amen. It is done!"

Archangel Uriel (Light of God/Fire of God)

Archangel Uriel is one of the seven archangels of the divine light presence whose important celestial frequency embodies God's divine peace, ministration, and service. This extraordinary angel is personally involved in helping each soul to align with the Christ Light Consciousness alight within their higher-self nature that emanates from the greater universal current. Amplifying the light of God's wisdom within each soul is what ultimately brings the human soul inner peace and spiritual growth through deepened cosmic consciousness. Archangel Uriel is also known as Saint Uriel and is often depicted in art with an open hand holding a flame, which signifies the divine light of God. Other symbolic associations with Archangel Uriel include him carrying a book or scroll, representing divine light knowledge.

Divine Light Message

"Relationships are a constant within your life, and the forging of honest and happy relationships is important for your soul's comfort and growth. You cannot forge longstanding relationships without harmony and understanding, and this requires an unconditionally loving and peaceful heart. You are being guided to bring peaceful resolution back into any inharmonious relationships you have with others that are special to your soul. While it can be emotionally difficult for you when your closest friends and loved ones fall short of their loyalty and support, and temporarily let you down, it is important to be able to let go of these human errors so that unconditional love can again prevail. This is all part of the tapestry of life and helps you to learn spiritual lessons rooted in love, compassion, understanding, forgiveness, and reverence. We want you to recognize how important it is to give gratitude for your relationships, for whether good or testing, there is a true blessing in all of them. Through this loving prayer, you will gain the spiritual light you require to help bring peace and harmony within your relationship once more. We angels will help you to perceive old arguments, disagreements, and emotional hurts in a higher light without the need for your righteousness and perfectionism to correct them. This deeper unconditional understanding of the spiritual light that you already share with each other, withstanding the shadow natures of you both, will invite divine love directly into your union to restore harmony, peace, and joy. We the angels are not only forging new relationships with you, but we are also guiding the right relationships to you so that you may learn to love and live in harmony with others. We are also helping you to forge a stronger relationship with your own divine nature so you unconditionally love and accept yourself as a perfect light of God."

Resistance Healing Prayer with Archangel Michael
(To help free you from energetic resistance to live your truth)

"Archangel Michael, please light up my consciousness with God's perfect truth, courage, and divine power. I allow the light to help me overcome all fear and resistance to living my truth and following my heart. I willingly release *this energetic resistance to the light and replace it with divine courage, truth, and harmony. I am ready to live my life to my greatest potential with truth in my heart and the creative light of my soul shining brightly. Thank you. Amen. It is done!"*

Archangel Michael (He who is like God)

Archangel Michael is probably the most famous and universally known archangel of them all. His magnificent celestial body is the divine expression of God's power, absolute truth, and protection. He is depicted in great works of art as a mighty angelic being who carries a protective shield and powerful sword of light, often referred to as the "sword of truth." Some have called him a warrior angel because of the biblical reference to his casting down the fallen angel, Lucifer. Archangel Michael can help us to slay the fears of our shadow nature, to break through our illusionary limitations with the power of God's truth, and to overcome our weaknesses with divine courage and fortitude. The divine light power bestowed on this astonishing archangel by God is truly remarkable. When we reach out to him for help, he will instantly intervene and guide us through our most ardent struggles, and will divinely protect us in all our ways.

Divine Light Message

"Resistance is nothing more than a delayed response to keep you from achieving that which you would truly and consciously love to experience. Resistance can also be perceived as a form of self-sabotage that can prevent you from experiencing possible failure or success when you feel you are unable to cope with it. Nonresistance is your path to spiritual freedom, and now is your opportunity to regain some glorious freedom and spread your symbolic angel wings and fly. Resistance is the ego's way of keeping you rooted to the material world to try and find answers to your concerns there without thinking and looking to a higher power for guidance. Nonresistance brings inner peace and surrender so that divine love can flow unhindered with ease and grace to intervene and help you. There are many times that you put up energetic barriers due to your unresolved fears and concerns, and so you resist that which would be good for you to experience. It is time to pay attention to the true expression of your heart and soul, and be fearless in your nonresistance to change. When you pray this purposeful prayer of healing resistance, know that you will become empowered with divine courage, insight, and fortitude to break through any barriers of resistance, both seen and unseen, that have previously held you back. We angels also help you to resist the temptations that are not in keeping with the lessons of the soul, which can be detrimental to your health, vitality, and creative power. The path of nonresistance to living your truth and following your heart is one that will bring you the greatest joy."

S

Self-Love Prayer with Archangel Chamuel (To help you love and approve of yourself)

"Archangel Chamuel, please light up my consciousness with God's rose pink divine light frequency of His perfect love. I allow the light to help soften my heart energy and alter my false perceptions so that I can become more gentle and kind toward myself. I willingly choose to resolve my negative, self-critical talk and limiting beliefs that I have accepted as real, and to replace them with the healing harmony of divine love. I accept that God loves me, and therefore I choose to love, approve of, and accept myself. Thank you. Amen. It is done!"

Archangel Chamuel (He who sees God/He who seeks God)

Archangel Chamuel is an astonishingly radiant angel who is the beautiful embodiment of God's all-powerful divine love. His remarkable angelic service

is to continuously out-ray God's divine love to all of humanity to help us overcome and rise above the illusionary fear of worldly appearances and false judgments. Divine love is at the origin of our being, and Archangel Chamuel inspires us to recognize and observe the divinity within ourselves and within all souls, and to express unconditional love for our self and others. Divine love is the most powerful cosmic force within the universe that can help to awaken us to the oneness and unity of creation, so that what we personally create is beneficial for the whole. It is the spectacular light that enables us to evolve our human souls to experience greater dimensions of light and consciousness.

Divine Light Message

"You are an exquisite soul with such profound spiritual beauty that the light you express is like a brilliant sun, an illuminating moon, and the brightest twinkling shining stars. You are a fascinating universe of light within your own physical form, and the magnitude of your beauty is carefully hidden from your conscious awareness because you would not be able to comprehend the power and glory of your own light within this earthly dimension. You were created from the heart and mind of God as a being of pure love with unlimited potential. The divine love that you are exists as a holy light that is the spiritual essence of your soul. Love is your true nature, your real self, and it is your best attribute. You needed to know this today because you have temporarily forgotten your extraordinary beauty, and you have presently accepted yourself as much less than you truly are. God delights when you rediscover your own inner beauty and true origin. Self-examination in a loving and unconditional way to help you initiate positive changes is far more appropriate for your soul than you condemning yourself with guilt, blame, and feelings of self-hatred. You are so much more than your character, personality, and shadow nature. You are a brilliant being of divine love, and expanding this love within you is the answer to total and complete fulfillment."

Surrender Prayer with Archangel Faith (To help you surrender your personal struggles and issues to God)

"Archangel Faith, please light up my mind, body and soul with God's royal blue divine light frequency of His perfect faithfulness. I allow the light to help me overcome my doubts as I completely surrender my fears and concerns over to God, to be dealt with in His perfect way. I am willing to stay in faith and let divine intelligence guide me in all my ways to bring about positive resolution. Thank you. Amen. It is done!"

Archangel Faith (Divine Complement of Archangel Michael)

Archangel Faith is the impressive divine feminine complement of the magnificent Archangel Michael.

This delightful archangel, sometimes referred to as Archeia Faith, in reference to her feminine nature, is the grand celestial embodiment of God's unwavering faithfulness. Archangel Faith also works with the royal blue divine light frequency of God's will and truth. She is significantly important in helping humanity to keep their faith in the light of God within them to overcome all physical world illusions and struggles. Archangel Faith can help us personally to release our doubts, to surrender our fears, and to ignite our hope and faith in God's divine light intelligence.

Divine Light Message

"As you experience challenges and obstacles in your daily life that you can't seem to overcome by only looking to the material world for help, then use this divine prayer of surrender to bring in the light of guidance that you need. Many of your problems continue without resolution because they are not completely surrendered into the light of a higher power, whether this be the higher power of your own God consciousness or the higher power of the celestial realm and Source. Your own interference is often aligned with the vibrations of doubt, fear, resistance, and lack of patience. Surrendering all of your doubts, fears, and insecurities about your main concern will immediately begin to create the vibrational space for divine light to enter and bring about perfect resolution in harmony with the synchronicity of divine timing. When you feel that there is no way out of a difficult situation and you have lost your hope and faith, then you can surrender this limiting belief to the angels because there are always divine solutions for all physical life concerns. The divine light will bring you to a greater clarity of mind and will illuminate the correct path that you need to take to assist you in overcoming your personal dilemma. When you surrender, you are asking a higher power for divine intervention, and you will always be shown the way and given the answers you seek to move forward. So look toward a spiritual solution today and surrender your plight to a higher power, as the result of your surrender will surely reap divine rewards."

Teenager Guidance/Protection Prayer with Archangel Michael
(To help you light up your teenager's life with divine guidance and protection)

"Archangel Michael, please send God's royal blue divine light frequency to positively influence and protect my teenage son/daughter (state their name) for his/her greatest good in accordance with his/her soul's plan. Let your powerful light protect him/her each day by steering him/her away from all harmful intentions and suggestions, both conscious and unconscious. Let the all-powerful light guide him/her in divine truth so that he/she continuously follows the path of his/her higher self, and will not be led astray by toxic influences. May his/her teenage years and beyond be blessed with divine insight, love, and protection with ease and grace. Thank you. Amen. It is done!"

Archangel Michael (He who is like God)

Archangel Michael is probably the most famous and universally known archangel of them all. His magnificent celestial body is the divine expression of God's power, absolute truth, and protection. He is depicted in great works of art as a mighty angelic being who carries a protective shield and powerful sword of light, often referred to as the "sword of truth." Some have called him a warrior angel because of the biblical reference to his casting down the fallen angel, Lucifer. Archangel Michael can help us to slay the fears of our shadow nature, to break through our illusionary limitations with the power of God's truth, and to overcome our weaknesses with divine courage and fortitude. The divine light power bestowed on this astonishing archangel by God is truly remarkable. When we reach out to him for help, he will instantly intervene and guide us through our most ardent struggles, and will divinely protect us in all our ways.

Divine Light Message

"Divine light will surround your teenager as they move into an exciting new life phase of soul expression that also involves the delicate state of hormonal changes and sensitivity of being. We have heard your pleas for divine intervention, and where appropriate and in accordance with their soul's lessons, we angels will always intervene and help. Teenagers by their very nature are going through a natural process of learning how to handle their own creative freedom and power. While it is necessary for them to learn from their own energetic mistakes so they can grow in psychological, emotional, and spiritual maturity, at times their free-will choices may not be in harmony with their soul's life purpose. We angels will then intervene and help to illuminate their consciousness with divine guidance so they can willfully choose right behavior and action accordingly. They must utilize the power of their own free will to positively change, and this is why your prayers of light can be so beneficial to empower their consciousness to do so. If you have a teenager who is presently troubled or in trouble, know that the divine light will always intervene to help bring them back to the true path of their soul's life purpose. Divine protection will also work behind the scenes of their life to remove any destructive influence of those who can easily manipulate a newly awakening consciousness. Whilst some experiences that you deem negative do teach the teenage soul many lessons, we angels still carefully watch over them to ensure they are not tempted by unenlightened forces or to make foolhardy leaps into murky, dangerous waters. Do not give up on the length of time it takes for your teenager to come into the light of their own creative potential; the power of prayer is consistently helping their consciousness to transform before you can observe the physical results. We carry your heartfelt prayers of love in our celestial light, and we blend them together to shine the love and light upon your child so that they are divinely guided and protected."

Thanksgiving Affirmation Prayer
(I AM Divine Decrees)
(To affirm gratitude for your blessings through your own divine authority)

"I love you, God. I love my life. Thank you, God.
I Am thankful for (state list of what you are
grateful for).

The Christ Light Consciousness

The Christ Light Consciousness is the pure divine
light intelligence and love that God embodies for
the whole of creation that illuminates and radiates
throughout the entire universe. The Christ Light
Consciousness is also a spectacular aspect of every
human soul, no matter what stage of spiritual awakening and maturity they are in, or what religion, if any,
they are personally aligned with. The divine aspect
that is known as the Christ Light Consciousness is
the spark of divine presence that exists within every
human soul. It is impossible to be without this God
consciousness because our individual souls of light
are all birthed from the One primordial ray of God's
Divine Light. It is the Light of Lights that weaves us all
together in the oneness of Creation. We carry God's
consciousness as the higher part of our soul nature
to help awaken and illuminate us, to evolve our souls
in harmony with divine truth and divine love.

Divine Light Message

"Repeat this effective affirmative prayer daily and as often as you feel intuitively called to because when you say it sincerely and from your heart, you will invoke immense spiritual power to continuously bless you. You are speaking powerful vibrational words of light over your yourself, your health, and your life each time you repeat this prayer. These words of light will directly intervene in your life and provide you with the vitality and blessings you have already affirmed. By being thankful for God, you instantly affirm your inseparable connection that is eternal, and you invoke the power of your own divine authority of the spirit of God within you to overcome the world of matter. By being thankful for your life, you help to empower the vital radiance of your physical energy and creative power, to cocreate your soul's light within the world through a healthy body and joyful spirit. By being thankful for the blessings that you have today, you will continue to be blessed through your sincere and humble gratitude in harmony with universal law. You have the gift of life and divine love in your heart, therefore you are abundant beyond your wildest dreams. Count your blessings with gratitude each day upon waking. Take a moment to breathe in the energy of gratitude and feel it with every breath. Think about all the things in your life, great and small, that you can be thankful for, and feel the presence of gratitude bloom within your heart. Let the love of gratitude permeate every cell of your body. You can expand your consciousness through growing in gratitude and love."

Travel Prayer with Archangel Raphael (To help you receive divine protection during travel)

"Archangel Raphael, please accompany me on my travels and divinely protect me with God's holy light to keep me safe in all my endeavors. I allow the light to inspire and guide my intuitive awareness so that I can make wise decisions for my greatest good. Please place your careful watch and protection over my belongings and bless my trip with God's perfect healing power to keep me vital and strong throughout all circumstances. Thank you. Amen. It is done!"

Archangel Raphael (God heals)

Archangel Raphael is typically known as God's divine healing angel who delivers God's all-powerful healing light to all who call on him for spiritual assistance. Another interpretation of his name is "God has healed," which suggests that health is already a firm reality within the mind and sight of God, and we consistently maintain this reality of perfect health within our true divine origin. Archangel Raphael's powerful divine light is therefore administered to help us to realign with our already-healed and healthy divine self. His beautiful divine light frequency also embodies the celestial qualities of divine abundance and spiritual protection during travel. He holds the complete wisdom of divine healing science within his consciousness and is therefore able to help anyone to develop and tap into their own internal divine healer, should they desire to understand the deeper truths of healing.

Divine Light Message

"The moment you ask a higher power for divine protection, it is given to you. You have used the power of your own divine authority to invite God's protective light to accompany you during your travels, and this shall be so. As you begin your journey, know that you will be divinely watched over and will be intuitively guided at times to subtly shift certain plans. A few minutes' delay here, a coffee stop there are just some of the multitude of ways in which we angels will reach and influence your consciousness to spiritually direct you with ease and grace. Cast the insecure and irrational fears of your travels aside and allow the light of God's protection and guidance to be the divine insurance that will help make your journey a successful and enjoyable one, whether it be for business or pleasure. Pray the prayer of travel from your heart and soul, and know that we have already answered. You will reach your destination, wherever it may be, and you will be held safe in angels' wings."

U

Unconditional Love Prayer with Archangel Chamuel
(To help amplify the power of unconditional love within you)

"Archangel Chamuel, please light up my heart's energy center with God's rose pink divine light frequency of His perfect love. I allow the light to gently lead me to a place deep within me where I can begin to resolve the emotional pain that has temporarily suppressed the pure light of my soul's true unconditional nature. I willingly choose to express unconditional love and compassion for myself and others in thought, word, and action. Thank you. Amen. It is done!"

Archangel Chamuel (He who sees God/He who seeks God)

Archangel Chamuel is an astonishingly radiant angel who is the beautiful embodiment of God's all-powerful divine love. His remarkable angelic service

is to continuously out-ray God's divine love to all of humanity to help us overcome and rise above the illusionary fear of worldly appearances and false judgments. Divine love is at the origin of our being, and Archangel Chamuel inspires us to recognize and observe the divinity within ourselves and within all souls, and to express unconditional love for our self and others. Divine love is the most powerful cosmic force within the universe that can help to awaken us to the oneness and unity of creation, so that what we personally create is beneficial for the whole. It is the spectacular light that enables us to evolve our human souls to experience greater dimensions of light and consciousness.

Divine Light Message

"Unconditional love is the soul's ability to love without conditions, and we angels have heard your heart's prayer to express a deeper level of unconditional love. God loves you unconditionally; we, the angels, love you unconditionally; and so we gladly lead you to a place within your consciousness where you can relearn to love yourself and others unconditionally. This place is the divine origin of your soul's true unconditional nature. Jesus Christ was a shining example of divine light regarding unconditional love, compassion, and forgiveness. It mattered not to him whether the individual was unenlightened as he saw only the divine presence within everyone. Will you open your spiritual eyes to see the divine presence everywhere? No matter what or whom you have issue with, they, like you, are a child of the divine. Loving unconditionally is not easy. It must come with spiritual knowledge, wisdom, and understanding. Know that we angels are helping to open your heart's energy frequency more and more so that you can recognize the divine light in all human souls behind the ego's shadows. You are truly evolving spiritually as you learn to love without conditions, and we celebrate your glorious divine light emanation throughout the celestial realms."

Unhappiness/Depression Healing Prayer with
Archangel Raziel
(To help you spiritually overcome your
unhappiness and depression)
"Archangel Raziel, please light up my consciousness with God's rainbow-ray light frequency of His perfect divine intelligence. I allow the light to release, correct, and help me resolve all errors in consciousness that have hindered my divine light expression and caused a depressurization in my energy flow. I willingly choose to monitor my thoughts and to quickly bring them back into harmony with divine love whenever they are focused elsewhere. I now choose to live my truth and follow my heart's lead without fear of failure and without allowing other people to interfere with my decisions. Thank you. Amen. It is done!"

Archangel Raziel (Secret of God)

This marvelous archangel is the legendary subject of the Book of the Angel Raziel, which is said to contain secret knowledge. He is imbued with remarkable divine wisdom and is the keeper of knowledge, mysteries of the world, and the secrets of God. His divine light frequency embodies all seven rays of divine light combined as one extraordinary light emanation signifying the rainbow ray. The divine light intelligence of the rainbow ray can reveal to us the divine knowledge we require to help us navigate our human soul through our physical incarnation in harmony with our life's plan. Archangel Raziel can help to illuminate our spiritual journey back into the realms of light and God consciousness.

Divine Light Message

"You are presently moving back into greater harmony with your own divine spark. The radiant joy of your soul has always existed within your consciousness and has truly never left you; it has only been temporarily shadowed over until now. Through this important divine healing prayer, we angels will help to uplift you and to amplify that spark of joy within you that is the eternal flame of God's essence and light. The illumination of this light will eventually burst through the shadows of your depression so that you will once again radiate vital energy, truth, happiness, and love. You are stronger than you realize, and you can overcome any physical life condition through the dynamic power of your own divine light empowered by the magnificent divine light of God that we angels bring to you. It is time for you to break free from the prison of darkness that has only ever held an illusionary grip over you. Take notice of how you are being gently encouraged and guided in your daily life to help free yourself from all previous restrictions. Divine intelligence is working God's perfect order through your consciousness, helping to correct any errors that you are willfully ready to resolve. Become more mindful of how you impact the quality of your own energy through the powerful frequency of your thoughts, beliefs, and actions, or lack of actions, and you will eventually overcome your struggle with unhappiness. There is no need for you to stay spiritually stuck any longer and to feel continuously unhappy and depressed. It is time for you to regain the pure joy of your soul's light."

V

Victory Prayer with Archangel Sandalphon (To help you affirm a victorious mindset and outcome)

*"Archangel Sandalphon, please bless my prayer
of victory with God's radiant divine light. I allow
the light to work with me in perfect cocreation
to help me achieve victory and success in (state
area you desire a victory) for my greatest good.
I declare through the power of my own divine
authority that I am already victorious. I now
release any energetic interference within my
consciousness that may sabotage my victory to
the divine light to be completely dissolved and
resolved. Thank you. Amen. It is done!"*

Archangel Sandalphon (co-brother with Archangel Metatron)

Archangel Sandalphon is considered to be the prophet Elijah who transformed his soul consciousness into the elevated status of an archangel upon entering the realms of light. He is also known as the twin or co-brother of the powerful Archangel Metatron, who was originally the human soul Enoch before he too became an archangel of cosmic consciousness. This astonishing archangel is said to be extremely tall, whose height, also symbolic for consciousness, stretches from the earth to the heavenly worlds of light. Archangel Sandalphon is known for his ability to gather the prayer requests of the faithful, to bless and arrange them in the divine light of his radiant celestial frequency, and to deliver them to God so they become empowered realized blessings for those who pray. He is also known as a master of heavenly song and is therefore associated with musical tones and vibrations, assisting in the glorious song of creation.

Divine Light Message

"This is your time for victory, so stay in patient faith as the divine light will assist you in the fulfillment of your heart's desire in God's perfect way. You have overcome certain obstacles and barriers that have previously held you back, and the divine light is helping to illuminate any final shadows of interference so that you immediately deal with them and have a clear path to success. You are already victorious as a divine spark of God, and the power of this victorious you, is brightly alight within the divine authority of your I AM presence. Affirming your victory in prayer will empower the creative spirit within you to blossom into your physical reality. Your prayer is being blessed with divine intelligence to help you cocreate your victory in harmony with your greatest good and the greater good of the whole. You can become victorious in all of your endeavors whenever your heart and soul are in perfect alignment with one another. We angels of divine light are overjoyed at the victory we can see before you. Take strength and comfort in knowing that your perseverance is about to spiritually and physically pay off as you will soon reach the pinnacle of your victory. Take your imaginary place on the spiritual podium of victory as we angels love to celebrate your achievements with you in the heavenly realms of light."

Vows/Contracts/Curses Release Prayer with Archangel Michael (To help override and transform any misuse of creative energy)

"Archangel Michael, please light up my consciousness and my soul's timeline with God's royal blue divine light frequency of His perfect truth and power. I allow the light of truth to reach deep into the origin of all conscious and unconscious destructive vows/contracts and curses that I myself or others have initiated and rightly correct or destroy them. I willingly choose to forgive myself and any others for their misuse of creative energy, and I bring this positive transformation into the present moment for my greatest good. Thank you. Amen. It is done!"

Archangel Michael (He who is like God)

Archangel Michael is probably the most famous and universally known archangel of them all. His magnificent celestial body is the divine expression of God's power, absolute truth, and protection. He is depicted in great works of art as a mighty angelic being who carries a protective shield and powerful sword of light, often referred to as the "sword of truth." Some have called him a warrior angel because of the biblical reference to his casting down the fallen angel, Lucifer. Archangel Michael can help us to slay the fears of our shadow nature, to break through our illusionary limitations with the power of God's truth, and to overcome our weaknesses with divine courage and fortitude. The divine light power bestowed on this astonishing archangel by God is truly remarkable. When we reach out to him for help, he will instantly intervene and guide us through our most ardent struggles, and will divinely protect us in all our ways.

Divine Light Message

"Vows and contracts that are not sealed in the spirit and harmony of divine truth do not align with the light of God and are therefore unreal from a higher sense perception. In the denser vibration of physical life, the effects of this misaligned destructive energy can still interfere with your health and life while an aspect of your consciousness has accepted the reality as true. Angry curses and evil words spoken are also depleted in light and truth, and can be detrimental to your vitality and creative power if they are subconsciously accepted as having power over you. Do not fear the misguided curses and words of another that create lies of ignorance because when you consciously shine the divine light of truth in its place, they will crumble and hold no power over you. Through this potent prayer, the royal blue divine light frequency will replace all that is insincere and impure within your consciousness so that you can regain your vital freedom and take back your creative power from the illusionary energetic interference. No one in this world or the next can hold any negative power over you when you reclaim the magnificent power of your own divine authority. The absolute power of the God, alive within you, thwarts all that is dark and misaligned in intention and will enable you to overcome any interference. The light of divine truth will override all negative and binding ties so that divine harmony can take place in your consciousness in God's perfect way.

Workplace Harmony Prayer with Archangel Uriel
(To help restore harmony in the workplace)

*"Archangel Uriel, please light up the combined
consciousness of my workplace with God's
divine light frequency of His perfect peace. I ask
that divine peace influence all who work there
to be more kind, considerate, and respectful of
one another. May the light of God's peace help
us to harmonize all of our energies together
productively so that creativity, quality service,
and great works can prevail. I ask that this
prayer be released for the greatest good of the
whole. Thank you. Amen. It is done!"*

Archangel Uriel (Light of God/Fire of God)

Archangel Uriel is one of the seven archangels of
the divine light presence whose important celestial
frequency embodies God's divine peace, ministration,
and service. This extraordinary angel is personally

involved in helping each soul to align with the Christ Light Consciousness alight within their higher-self nature that emanates from the greater universal current. Amplifying the light of God's wisdom within each soul is what ultimately brings the human soul inner peace and spiritual growth through deepened cosmic consciousness. Archangel Uriel is also known as Saint Uriel and is often depicted in art with an open hand holding a flame, which signifies the divine light of God. Other symbolic associations with Archangel Uriel include him carrying a book or scroll, representing divine light knowledge.

Divine Light Message

"The environment in which you work can become inharmonious when one or more people who work there interfere with the group dynamics through their own internal conflict. Conflict is a message for the human soul that it is time to realign their energies back into harmony with divine love. If you are presently experiencing conflict within the workplace, then this practical prayer will help to shine the divine light of peace into the group so that harmony can again be restored for the greatest good of the whole. Some people may end up leaving the group and move on to new beginnings elsewhere, while others will join who are more agreeable to the group's combined energies and intentions so that harmony can once more prevail. It is important for you to be happy and contented in the work that you do for you to be of sincere creative service. When you give your best, no matter what job or career you do, then you are setting a standard of excellent service that will not go unnoticed by God. In your future, golden doors of opportunity will open for you due to your own dedication and quality of service. There are times in your work life for you to naturally reap and sow, so keep in mind that while you may be experiencing difficult times, this is only temporary. You will eventually come to reap the golden fruit of your well-deserved blessings."

World Blessing Prayer with Archangel Michael
(To help send divine light to the world)

"Archangel Michael, please light up the whole world with God's royal blue divine light frequency of His perfect protection and power. Send the highest forces of divine light to any earthly disaster and to where it is most needed to help restore harmony, peace, and order where there has been destruction and disruption. Please bless the combined consciousness of humanity with the divine light of truth to help each soul awaken and willfully choose peace and unity with all. Thank you. Amen. It is done!"

Archangel Michael (He who is like God)

Archangel Michael is probably the most famous and universally known archangel of them all. His magnificent celestial body is the divine expression of God's power, absolute truth, and protection. He is depicted in great works of art as a mighty angelic being who carries a protective shield and powerful sword of light, often referred to as the "sword of truth." Some have called him a warrior angel because of the biblical reference to his casting down the fallen angel, Lucifer. Archangel Michael can help us to slay the fears of our shadow nature, to break through our illusionary limitations with the power of God's truth, and to overcome our weaknesses with divine courage and fortitude. The divine light power bestowed on this astonishing archangel by God is truly remarkable. When we reach out to him for help, he will instantly intervene and guide us through our most ardent struggles, and will divinely protect us in all our ways.

Divine Light Message

"Any sincere prayer said on behalf of the world, the earth's resources, and mankind is a true blessing of light that certainly makes a positive difference in the world and within the combined consciousness of humanity. When the majority of humanity awakens to the truth of unity and love, then more light and power will be released upon the earth from the higher realms of light to greatly assist in human soul and world ascension. The world and her resources are continuously evolving and adapting, and the light from your prayers helps to support and empower this natural creative process. When earthly disasters and trauma affect the world, then God's light and power will intervene there for the greatest good of the whole. It is your prayers for the world that helps to anchor God's light there, and therefore they are truly invaluable. One prayer joins another soul's prayer to continuously build into a ball of light that creates a huge wave of power to sweep through the atmosphere of the world and to settle exactly where help is most needed. We thank you for your world blessing and creative participation in the ongoing evolution of God's miraculous and beautiful world."

X

*X-Ray Intuitive Vision Prayer with
Archangel Raphael
(To help you develop divine insight)*
*"Archangel Raphael, please light up my third-
eye energy center with God's emerald green
divine light frequency to help awaken my soul's
divine insight for my greatest good. I willingly
allow the light to clear all false perceptions that
interfere with the full clarity, understanding, and
expression of my intuitive vision. I acknowledge
my intuition as a natural divine ability of my soul
to help me receive intuitive visions and insight
from God, the angels, and my higher self to assist
me in all my ways. Thank you. Amen. It is done!"*

Archangel Raphael (God heals)

Archangel Raphael is typically known as God's
divine healing angel who delivers God's all-powerful
healing light to all who call on him for spiritual assistance. Another interpretation of his name is "God

has healed," which suggests that health is already a firm reality within the mind and sight of God, and we consistently maintain this reality of perfect health within our true divine origin. Archangel Raphael's powerful divine light is therefore administered to help us to realign with our already-healed and healthy divine self. His beautiful divine light frequency also embodies the celestial qualities of divine abundance and spiritual protection during travel. He holds the complete wisdom of divine healing science within his consciousness and is therefore able to help anyone to develop and tap into their own internal divine healer, should they desire to understand the deeper truths of healing.

Divine Light Message

"The gentle awakening of your higher intuitive nature involves you releasing limiting perceptions that have no light of truth within them so that you can receive a greater expansion of light intelligence. This intuitive development prayer will help to bring to mind the interfering perceptions that you are presently ready to correct and let go of. In doing so, you will begin to create the space within your consciousness to allow more divine insight and visions of truth to be revealed to you. Intuition begins to develop within the human soul at a denser level of vibration that is often called the gut instinct until a mixture of life experience and spiritual growth enables the soul's light to mature and receive deeper divine insight. Divine insight flows from the heart and mind of God (truth and love), through your higher self, the archangels, and your guardian angel in perfect ways that will suit your level of soul development. You are required to do your part to develop your divine intuitive nature through the active use of prayer, meditation, and mindfulness practice, along with spiritual study and contemplation. The divine light frequency will work in perfect harmony with your conscious participation to bring greater clarity of mind and divine vision to you."

Y

Youthful Body/Mind Prayer with Archangel Gabriel
(To help keep you vital, strong, and joyful)

"Archangel Gabriel, please light up my consciousness with God's pure white divine light frequency of His perfect purity, joy, and vitality. I allow the light of divine intelligence to help me regenerate a youthful radiant and vital body in alignment with my perfect original divine design. I declare that my body is vital and strong. My mind is clear and bright. My appearance is youthful and glowing. My soul resonates with the holy divine spark of God. Youthfulness and regeneration is consciously being projected in my DNA. Thank you. Amen. It is done!"

Archangel Gabriel (God is my strength)

Archangel Gabriel is a remarkable messenger angel who appears in both the Old and New Testaments of the Holy Bible, although he is not directly referred to as an archangel. Known as the angel of revelation and annunciation, Archangel Gabriel can help us to achieve clarity and purity of mind by revealing divine truth and intuitive understanding within our consciousness. Universally he is recognized as a very important divine messenger of God, especially as he announces the planned births of John the Baptist and Jesus Christ. This magnificent archangel can help us to communicate the divine light expression of our soul in a harmonious and pure manner. Archangel Gabriel is intimately connected to harmonizing the divine feminine within all souls, and his divine light frequency also assists all those who desire help with conception, pregnancy, and the welfare of children.

Divine Light Message

"You are always vital, strong, and a perfect picture of health and wholeness within the heart and mind of God. This youthful body/mind healing prayer will help you to realign with the highest version of you so that the grand reflection of your perfect self can be filtered down and projected in your conscious awareness. The results of this out-picturing will begin to create subtle and profound shifts in your waking consciousness that will guide your self-awareness to make necessary and positive life changes that will help to revitalize you. The pure white light frequency of God's divine intelligence supports your energy body with a network of instructions that helps to restructure, repair, and resolve any dysfunction within it that is causing physical disarray, decay, and accelerated aging. Divine instructions are always given in harmony with your soul's purpose and any karmic influences you may be working through. It is time for you to take more conscious responsibility of your own energy to help positively support your physiology with vital power. Allow the white light to bring purity and joy to your thoughts, emotions, and actions to help you regain a more vital and youthful presence of being. True joy of the soul that is able to radiate with ease and grace through the waking consciousness without restriction is the divine answer to vital health and longevity."

Z

Zodiacal Light Prayer with Archangel Metatron (To help you receive divine light from the cosmic consciousness)

"Archangel Metatron, please light up my consciousness with pure cosmic light and life-force power gathered from the abundant streams of God's zodiacal light rays. I willingly accept this cosmic light to help empower my divine creative expression, to increase my vitality, and to illuminate my soul with divine intelligence. Let the planets and stars twinkle and shine their cosmic power directly upon my human soul to help reveal the hidden depths of my unlimited divine potential. Thank you. Amen. It is done!"

Archangel Metatron

Archangel Metatron maintains celestial charge over the brilliant light source in the heavenly cosmos where his face is said to be more dazzling than the sun. He is known by some sources as the chancellor of heaven who also serves as a celestial scribe. This astonishingly powerful angel is considered to be amongst the highest of the angels and is the embodiment of ancient knowledge and cosmic wisdom. Archangel Metatron is said to have been the prophet Enoch, the great grandfather of the biblical Noah, who through his spiritual enlightenment was then transformed into an angel upon his bodily ascension into heaven. He is associated as the co-brother of the Archangel Sandalphon due to their similar human-soul-to-angelic-light ascension status. Archangel Metatron is thought to perfectly understand the sacred geometric design of the cosmos and is an expert of soul ascension and light-body integration work.

Divine Light Message

"You are a noble and heroic soul who is travelling an extraordinary spiritual journey throughout time and space within the magnitude of the entire multiverse. The heavens and the earth support you wholly in your beautifully unique and individual adventure. Stars shine their cosmic light just for you to help perfectly illuminate your life's path. You are presently moving into a period of greater global awareness of who you truly are and of your remarkable creative potential. You are evolving rapidly in spiritual consciousness. It is time for you to take this next stage of your life in full power and splendor of your astonishing divine authority and creative expression. You are a divine star, so take your place right now in this earthly world and shine your light ever more brightly. This beautiful prayer is a wonderful prayer for you to say at nighttime whilst looking up at the moon and stars. Stand outside with your arms stretched high above your head and with your palms facing the heavens. You will receive a glorious boost of cosmic light and life-force power directly entering into your energy body to help revitalize you and to amplify your amazing creative power."

The End!

To find out more about Joanne, the angels, online healing courses, and workshops, you can visit her website at *www.joannebrocas.com*

$\mathcal{I}$ ndex

About the Author

Joanne Brocas is an angel expert, divine healer, and best-selling author of *The Power of Angels* and *The Power of Angel Medicine*, with more than two decades of experience in angelic communication and healing. As a small child, Joanne naturally and easily communicated with her guardian angel due to the consistent and daily use of the divine power of prayer, which helped her to establish and maintain a strong, clear, and open connection with the angelic realm throughout her life. She is a popular and regular guest on radio shows. Her articles have been featured in some of the world's leading healing magazines, and she is the divine healing columnist for *The Otherside Press*. Her angel healing books have been endorsed by several medical and energy-healing experts, and they have received exceptional critical acclaim by prominent reviewers. Born in South Wales, Joanne and her husband live in Orlando, Florida. She teaches board-approved healing programs and workshops internationally, as well as extremely popular online courses that enable others to study with her in the comfort of their own homes. Joanne can be reached via her Website, *www.joannebrocas.com*.